THE INNER GAME OF
RAISING PRIVATE MONEY

THE INNER GAME OF

RAISING PRIVATE MONEY

EFFECTIVE STRATEGIES AND ACTIONS FOR RAISING ALL THE PRIVATE MONEY YOU NEED AND WANT TO FUND YOUR INVESTMENT OPPORTUNITIES.

IMPLEMENTATION
SELF IMAGE
EXECUTION
PERSONAL EFFECTIVENESS
STRATEGIES & PRACTICES
SUPPORT PROGRAM

WILLIE C. HOOKS

XULON PRESS

Xulon Press
2301 Lucien Way #415
Maitland, FL 32751
407.339.4217
www.xulonpress.com

Xulon Press

© 2017 by Willie C. Hooks

All rights reserved solely by the author. The author guarantees all contents are original and do not infringe upon the legal rights of any other person or work. No part of this book may be reproduced in any form without the permission of the author. The views expressed in this book are not necessarily those of the publisher.

Printed in the United States of America.

Edited by Xulon Press.

ISBN-13: 9781545603291

The ability to raise money is a critical skill that will support you in achieving greater success and in building financial wealth much faster.

Regardless of the business that you are in, or the project that you are pursuing, you will need money and financial resources to capture that opportunity.

The Inner Game of Raising Private Money will support you in developing the Inner Game that is necessary to raise all the money you want, need, and require to fund your business, projects or opportunities.

Willie C. Hooks

CONTENTS

Introduction ix

Chapter One: The Inner Game of Raising Private Money 1
Chapter Two: The Raising Private Money Success Model 10
Chapter Three: Self-Image Psychology 20
Chapter Four: The Power of Beliefs 27
Chapter Five: Million Dollar Support Program 39
Chapter Six: Effective Money Communication 50
Chapter Seven: Elevate Your Raising Money Game 62
Chapter Eight: Identity Matrix: Who Are You 71
Chapter Nine: Creating a Winning Money Identity 82

Conclusions 103
Exercise Answers 105

INTRODUCTION

FOR THE PAST 15 YEARS, I have been training, coaching and consulting with real estate investors and real estate business owners, supporting them in their quest to build a financially successful business. During that time, I have worked with hundreds of real estate business owners, and, at some point, they all realize that they need to enhance their abilities to raise private money to take their business to the next financial level.

I use the term private money, because the money these real estate business owners require, typically comes from individuals and not financial institutions. In this dynamic economy, there are lots of individuals looking for alternatives to the traditional investment opportunities, such as investing in the stock market, or investing in large institutional funds. Therefore, the number of individuals and investors open to becoming private money sources are increasing, and this creates a huge opportunity for real estate investors.

So, if you are a real estate owner, a real estate entrepreneur, or thinking of becoming one, please answer the following questions because your answers will tell you, if this is the right book for you.

Are you tired of falling short of your goals for raising private money month after month?

Are you feeling frustrated because you have not been able to raise the amount of private money that you desire?

Are you experiencing stress or anxiety because you feel that by now you should have cracked the code that would allow you to generate the amount of private money that you need?

Are you ashamed or disappointed when you look at the meager amount you have raised in the past year?

Are you afraid that you will not be able to live the lifestyle that you desire because your financial future is dependent on your ability to raise private money, an activity that you are currently failing in?

Are your business colleagues concerned because you are falling far short of fulfilling your responsibilities and meeting your company goals for raising private money?

Are you feeling disappointed with yourself because you know what to do to raise more private money, but you're not doing it consistently?

Are you quick to come up with reasons and excuses in regard to why you are not achieving your goals for raising private money?

Are you procrastinating on following up on opportunities to raise private money because your fear of engaging in a conversation with new sources is too high?

Are you feeling like you're on a treadmill because you keep starting over again and again without getting any closer to achieving your private money goals?

Are you thinking about giving up on your goals for raising private money or about giving up on raising private money altogether?

If you answered, "Yes," to even a few of the questions above, then *The Inner Game of Raising Private Money* is the right book for you. In fact, it is a *must-read* because it will significantly change your raising private money results.

To be clear, the only reason that you should care about any of this is because without understanding and adjusting your Inner Game, you will *never* be able to consistently raise the amount of private money that you desire. Research shows that without addressing your Inner Game, you will continue to raise the same amount of private money that you have been raising—plus or minus 5 percent.

Understanding your Inner Game in regard to raising private money is critical, not because it is nifty and cool, but because it is the key to increasing your performance and accelerating your private money results.

If you want to accelerate your private money results and achieve a significant increase in the amounts of money that you raise, you must understand—and then address—any Inner Game challenges that you have.

Introduction

Yes, you have some Inner Game challenges that are preventing you from raising all the private money that you want, need, and desire. Check your financial performance and results over the past year. If you did not raise more private money than you need to take advantage of all the opportunities that you saw and all the other opportunities that you could have generated, you have some major Inner Game challenges to be resolved.

Your Inner Game is destructive and insidious because the chances are high that you do not even know it is the root cause of your underperformance, poor performance, and disappointing results. Additionally, instead of looking at your Inner Game, you will start to doubt yourself, invest in additional training programs, and/or adopt the practice of chronic procrastination to avoid timely follow-up on private money opportunities.

Here is a great example from one of my clients, Dan. Month after month, Dan was not achieving his raising private money goals. He knew that raising a million dollars of private money yearly would allow him to leverage opportunities that would provide the financial resources he needed to retire and ensure his family a wonderful lifestyle.

Clearly, Dan wanted the results that would come from achieving his private money goal. He would be one of the first to admit that his goal was achievable. However, even though Dan knew *conceptually* what to do to achieve his goal, he was not able to get himself to take actions consistently.

I said *"conceptually"* because unless you're taking the actions that you know you should be taking; you will only have the *concept* of what is required to raise more private money than you need. Experience and results only come from taking action. One of the major Inner Game challenges that private money raisers encounter is the inability to step out of what they know conceptually and step into taking consistent, committed action.

After completing just one of the exercises in *The Inner Game of Raising Private Money*, Dan became intimately aware of the fact that he was operating at a 30 percent effectiveness level with his activities and not the illusionary 90 percent level that he had imagined he was achieving.

The mantra in this book is "Increased performance and accelerated results, the key to raising all the private money that you need, want, and desire." In fact, understanding and adjusting your Inner Game is the secret to achieving a quantum increase in your performance and your private money results, as well as to achieving your ultimate life goals.

Chapter One

THE INNER GAME OF RAISING PRIVATE MONEY

REMEMBER THAT THERE WILL ALWAYS be two games you will be playing simultaneously with whatever goal or business results you are striving to reach. The first is the Outer Game, referring to the targeted goal you want to achieve. Success leaves clues, and the keys to that success with this first game is to use proven, winning strategies and follow best practices to achieve your objectives for raising private money.

While this book contains some effective outer-game strategies and best practices for raising private money, the Outer Game is not the focus here. By now you should have already gained knowledge in regard to raising private money from books, workshops, seminars, and your own practical experiences. This book addresses the proven fact that you will implement very little of what you have learned if you have not mastered the second game—your Inner Game.

A look to the world of sports helps us understand the Inner Game. Most athletes will tell you that 80 percent of their success is mental, referring to all that is going on inside their minds when participating and competing in their sport. This is no different from what you are experiencing with raising private money. What is going on inside your mind will impact your performance. In fact, your current attitude and beliefs about raising private money will influence your results significantly because what's happening in your mind will determine how effective you are at the Outer Game.

In this chapter we are going to look at what the Inner Game is, how to identify it, and how to overcome any challenges it presents, so you can maximize your potential, achieve your financial goals, and create the prosperous business that you desire.

Now is the time to learn how to refuse to let what is going on between your ears stop you from achieving the private money results you need, want, and desire.

When I was young, I saw a caterpillar turn into a cocoon and then from a cocoon, transform itself into a beautiful butterfly. I still hold that vivid and powerful image in my mind.

I love that butterfly transformation image because it really speaks to me about the potential you have to achieve your goals. In this particular case, I am talking about your potential to raise more private money than you are now. In fact, you have the potential to raise all the private money you need, want, and desire for your business and for your goals.

However, you are very much like the caterpillar, unsure of how to transform yourself into a butterfly. The caterpillar cannot imagine, or cannot see itself, crawling around on a leaf and one day transforming into a beautiful butterfly and then taking flight.

It is very much like this for many people who cannot see themselves as someone who could talk to busy professionals, high net worth individuals, and other private money sources. You may not see yourself as someone that could have a conversation and develop a high level of trust with a private money source. You may not see yourself as someone able to deliver a peak interest statement that generates excitement and inspires the other person to want to hear more about what you are doing, your opportunities, and how you can help them get what they want.

I like the metaphor of a transforming caterpillar because it speaks to me of the unseen potential that you have. You can take that potential that you have inside of you, that butterfly that you have inside, the one who has the ability to raise private money, by transforming from the cocoon and ultimately turning into an effective and powerful private money–raising butterfly.

This transformation allows you to soar and to be very successful at raising private money. You have that same potential in terms of raising private money inside of you, just as the caterpillar has the potential to emerge from a cocoon and ultimately transform into a beautiful winged butterfly taking flight. To use that potential, you must start on the inside.

Human behavior is very fascinating to me. Many times when I first encounter people interested in raising more private money, they have just completed a workshop or a training program where they learned the strategies and best practices to do that. Therefore, each of them knows and understands at various levels the mechanics, strategies, and practices for raising private money.

It is fascinating because, after all the training they have received on how to raise private money and many times even before they have tried to raise any money at all, I hear them say how difficult it will be for them.

Three magic questions come to mind. How do they know that raising private money will be their biggest challenge? How can they be so certain that raising private money will be the most difficult part of building a successful business? Finally, how can they predict that raising private money will be the one thing that will make them fail?

Then I ask, "Have you ever tried raising private money?"

When asked that question, 95 percent of the time the answer is, "No." They also have never tried implementing the winning strategies and best practices for raising private money that they have been taught. They just assume that raising private money will be the most difficult part of the process for them.

I then ask them, "How did you come up with the conclusion that raising private money will be hard for you?" And they answer, "I just know it will be hard for me. It will be difficult if not impossible."

The reality of their current belief structure is that raising private money will be difficult because of some assumptions created from past experience. They may not even be able to articulate clearly why they have this belief or where they got it. To be clear, their Inner Game communicates that message to them. That negative belief about their ability does not have anything to do with their true potential to raise all the private money they need, want, and desire.

When I ask them, "Do you think you could follow a script if I gave you one?" They all answered absolutely; with practice, they could follow a script. "Do you think that you could talk about your business opportunity in such a way that you could generate excitement?" Yes, they could.

One effective strategy in conversations is not to ask for the money. Another winning strategy for raising much *more* money is to remember that you are not there to sell or to convince the other person of anything. You are merely sharing what you do with excitement and enthusiasm while building relationships.

A very effective private fundraising success practice is to communicate and engage with people, with excitement, about what you are doing in such a way that people will ask you to tell them more. In reality, you are going to be more interested in understanding their situation and what they are trying to do. You want to understand and identify what their priorities are. This is not selling; you are not trying to force or convince them to purchase anything. Rather you are truly interested in them and what they are trying to achieve.

People often say they are afraid they will not be able to "sell" their idea to obtain investors. Others will say, "Why would anyone loan me money?"

Keep in mind, raising private money is not about getting someone to loan you money. Instead, it is about your ability to talk about what you are doing with excitement and building trusting relationships. When you shift the conversation from you to them and you become interested in what they are doing, you will discover their passions, interests, and aspirations.

When asked if they think that they are able to follow those practices for raising private money, everybody says, "Yes." Unfortunately, almost all of them continue to have a negative inner conversation, where once again they cannot visualize themselves being effective at raising private money.

That response is the heart of the Inner Game of raising private money. All the training in the world will not allow you to execute the winning strategies or best practices if you do not first start on the inside. Therefore, success in raising private money starts with your Inner Game. Until you can get that aligned with what you are trying to do, you can't use all that knowledge and experience about raising private money consistently.

In a moment, you will complete an exercise that enables you to truly get in touch with any Inner Game challenges and roadblocks about raising more private money. Take a moment to reflect on these questions:
1. Where do you feel uncomfortable in regard to raising private money? Whatever you are feeling is your own perception of raising private money, and therefore, it is totally in your control to change your perception.
2. What is the amount of private money—the number—that causes you to doubt your ability to raise that amount? Again, this is your own perception that you can change.
3. What activities or situations with raising private money make you uncomfortable? Discomfort creates procrastination and will cause you to be ineffective when talking with private money sources. Being uncomfortable will prevent you from delivering a peak interest statement that generates excitement within other people.

Let's complete the exercise. Please answer the series of questions below, responding honestly and openly. Do not think of this as a simple workbook exercise. Instead, know that this is an opportunity for you to truly understand what is going on inside you, inside your Inner Game—how you truly think about raising private money. This gives you an opportunity to see the barriers that are preventing you from achieving your private money goals. Please take this exercise seriously because the result provides some truly valuable life-changing information that will help you determine what makes you feel uncomfortable, thereby limiting the use of your full raising money potential.

Raising Private Money Exercise #1

Set a goal for the exact amount of private money that you will raise over the next two years. As you read the list of numbers representing that amount, take notice of what is going on in your mind and in your body. Also note any positive or negative emotions that surface.
What two-year private money goal makes you feel uncomfortable?

- Is it $10,000?
- Is it $50,000?
- Is it $100,000?
- Is it $500,000?
- Is it 1 million dollars?
- Is it 5 million dollars?
- Is it 10 million dollars?
- Is it 20 million dollars?
- Is it 50 million dollars?

Great. Now take a moment and write down your reaction to the exercise in a journal or notebook as you reflect on the following Reflective Assessment Questions:
  a. What positive or negative feelings or emotions did you experience?
  b. What positive or negative feelings or emotions did you have relative to any number or numbers?
  c. What were your thoughts about the dollar amounts?
  d. What insights did you gain, if any, from the exercise?
  e. What will you do with any insights that you gained from completing the exercise?

Raising Private Money Exercise #2

In this exercise you will go through an eyes-open, guided imagery process. As you do so, imagine yourself having a conversation with a busy professional or a high net worth individual. This person has already told you that they have a 5-million-dollar investment portfolio and that they are considering ways to diversify. You are well past your third contact with this person, so you are able to speak freely.

Do you have that high net worth person in mind? Can you visualize yourself about to have this discussion with them?

Okay, begin the conversation in your mind, visualizing yourself as you participate in a highly engaging discussion. As you're having this imaginary discussion, please answer a few questions, noticing what is going on within your mind and your body.

a. At what point do you start to feel some stress and tension about having a conversation with someone you think is important, someone with an investment portfolio in the millions?
b. At what point do you start to stutter?
c. At what point do you start to have doubts?
d. At what point does what's going on inside your head interfere with your actions?
e. At what point is your conversation affected by what's going on inside your mind?
f. What insights, if any, did you gain from the exercise?
g. What are you going to do differently as a result of completing the exercise?

Raising Private Money Exercise #3

Regardless of how or what you feel—stressed, doubtful, powerless—it is all happening in your Inner Game, in your mind. The thoughts, feelings, and emotions that are swirling around inside of you are impacting your performance. The reality is that what is going on in your head can support you or block you, making it impossible for you to reach your fullest potential at raising private money.

When you are in a potential money-raising situation and you perceive that you need to act or perform differently than you see yourself to be, your Inner Game kicks in and blocks you from using the effective strategies that will enable you to reach your goals for raising private money.

Take a moment and answer the following Reflective Assessment Questions concerning what private money areas you have difficulty with:
a. Do you feel comfortable raising $5,000 to $20,000 because you have had success in the past?
b. How do feel about approaching high net worth people and engaging in a conversation with them?
c. Do your fears emerge when you think about talking to business professionals or high net worth individuals?

d. Do you feel comfortable talking to your friends and family about private money but uncomfortable talking to busy professionals?
   e. Do you feel comfortable talking to busy professionals on the first contact, but uncomfortable on the third?
   f. What insights if any did you gain from the exercise?
   g. What are you going to do differently as a result of completing the exercise?

Note that negative internal feelings and thoughts of uncertainty will surface in spite of your potential for raising private money. You really have the potential to raise all the private money that you need to achieve success, but you must learn how to change your inner negative emotions.

Successful private money raisers come from a wide range of backgrounds and experiences. I see people who are successful raising private money with college and university degrees. I see people who are successful at raising private money who do not have degrees. I see successful people who are young and others who are older, all with a wide range of personalities. In fact, people who are successful at raising private money are quite a diverse group, coming from many walks of life.

Based on that assessment, I can say with a very high degree of certainty that you can raise private money and develop a successful business. I also feel comfortable saying that you have enough knowledge on how to raise private money to have a very productive and successful private money conversation.

The chances are very high that I have seen someone with your background, or one very similar to yours, be very successful at raising private money.

A major key to raising private money successfully lies in your ability to master your Inner Game about private money. The more you know about yourself and your Inner Game, the greater the chances are that you will use your Inner Game to unlock more of your potential for raising private money.

Reflective assessment questions like the ones you have answered are designed to help you uncover the blocks and barriers to reaching your fullest potential at raising private money. The more you know about what is going on inside your head, the sooner you can address your self-imposed limitations and move on to raise the money you need for your business.

Positive growth and change starts with answering reflective assessment questions. They allow you to see the self-imposed barriers and self-imposed limitations that cause you to procrastinate, to hesitate, and to be ineffective when having private money conversations.

Here is one more example of how your Inner Game impacts the use of your ability. Imagine a one-foot by forty-foot board is placed on the ground. You then stand on the board at one end, and your foot is wide enough that you should be able to stand comfortably on the board. Next, walk the length of the board—only forty feet—without falling off.

Do you get the visual? The challenge is simple. If you walk the forty feet to the other end of the board without falling off, I will give you all the private money that you need for your business for one full year.

You have all the potential to walk the forty feet without falling off because the board is wide enough to ensure your success.

Do you think you could do it? Now let's add one condition before you accept the agreement.

Instead of the board lying flat on the ground, it will be raised 100 feet in the air. Now imagine yourself standing on one end of the board, and you have to cross the forty feet without falling off.

Are you still willing to accept this challenge?

Note that your potential has not changed. You have the ability to easily walk across a forty-foot board because it is 1 foot wide. However, when the board is raised 100 feet in the air without a safety net, your Inner Game, the game inside your head, doesn't allow you to feel as comfortable as you did when the board was lying flat on the ground.

This is an excellent example because it clearly demonstrates the impact of your Inner Game on your performance, and how what is going on inside your mind can block the use of your full potential.

In the next chapter, I want to make sure that you clearly understand what I mean when I use the term Inner Game. I also want you to understand how your Inner Game impacts your ability to use your full potential to raise private money.

Chapter Two

THE RAISING PRIVATE MONEY SUCCESS MODEL

IN THIS CHAPTER, I AM going to ensure that you understand exactly what I mean when I use the terms Outer Game and Inner Game. This is important because I use the term Inner Game in a very specific and expansive way. In fact, I have developed a Raising Private Money Success Model that shows each component referred to when I say Outer Game or Inner Game. In addition, I am very sure that the way I use Outer Game and Inner Game is very different from anyone else's definition. This uniqueness is what makes the Raising Private Money Success Model so powerful and effective when it comes to teaching you how to use more of your potential to raise more private money and how to achieve financial success.

Understanding and implementing the Raising Private Money Success Model will help you achieve greater results.

I use a pyramid to represent the Raising Private Money Success Model. The Model has a pyramid which is divided into three components. The pyramid is also surrounded by a border. This basic image represents everything that you need to be, to do, or to have to achieve any goal for raising the private money you desire. You will see exactly what I mean as I explain each component of the Raising Private Money Success Model.

The Outer Game of Raising Private Money

The first component of the success model, the base of the inside pyramid, is the Outer Game, again referring to the goal you are trying to achieve. In this particular case, you are striving to raise more private money. Therefore, this component refers to the winning strategies and best practices for raising private money.

To be much more successful, you must understand and implement the winning strategies and best practices for raising private money.

I've included a partial list of the strategies and practices that you are taught to implement to be effective at the Outer Game of raising private money.

1. Knowing what to do and what to say the first time you talk to a private money source.
2. Knowing what to do and say the second time you talk to a private money source.
3. Knowing what to do and say the third time you talk to a private money source.
4. Knowing what to do before and after you talk with a private money source.
5. Knowing how to develop and cultivate the relationship with a private money source.
6. Knowing what to do and what to say when you are working in your warm market with people you already know.
7. Knowing how to generate excitement when you are talking to someone.
8. Knowing never, ever to ask for the money.
9. Knowing not to use the telling-and-selling approach when you are in a conversation with a private money source.
10. Knowing how to develop trust and how to create a foundation for influencing people.
11. Knowing how to use a conversation stack so that you strengthen your relationships with the people you meet.

Inner Game of Raising Private Money

The rest of the Raising Private Money Success Model is about the Inner Game.

The Inner Game consists of three core levels: Personal Effectiveness, Self-Image Psychology, and Private Money Coaching and Support. We will discuss each part of the Inner Game separately to ensure that you understand it and how to utilize your Inner Game to raise more private money.

The Personal Effectiveness stage is where you first encounter the human element blocking you from using your full potential, along with all the knowledge and techniques that you have learned from your studying, experiences, and training programs.

Here are just a few key questions that will help you understand your level of personal effectiveness at raising private money:

1. Are you clear about your private money goals?
2. Are you clear about your monthly, quarterly, and annual private money goals?
3. By when do you want to have raised the amount of private money that you desire?
4. Have you blocked off enough time each week for completing the activities needed to be successful at raising private money?
5. Are you procrastinating when it comes to making and keeping your private money fundraising commitments?

As anyone who understands the science behind goal achievement will tell you, you need to be very clear about your specific goals. In that way, you will see the information and opportunities that will support you in achieving your goals. If you don't have a clear goal of how much private money you want to raise, your subconscious mind may block the very information that you need to achieve your goal because it does not know what you want.

Remember the old saying, "If you don't know where you want to go, any road will take you there." The same is true of raising private money. If you don't have a clear goal of exactly how much private money you want to raise, and by when, you will not know if you are making progress toward it. And you will just walk around with this general feeling of not being successful at raising private money, which does not help you at all.

Without a clear goal and a defined period to achieve the result, it becomes easier and easier not to take action. In fact, it is very hard to maintain the drive and energy necessary to be successful without any definite target.

Being clear on your exact private money goal is critical for achieving success. However, it is not sufficient merely to be clear about the goal. You also need an action plan with the actual implementable steps that you will take to achieve your goal. For example, if your strategy is to achieve your goal by first working your warm market, you will need to create a plan to guide your actions, to keep you on track, and to ensure that you are making sufficient progress toward that goal.

A well-considered plan will put you into contact with people who are looking to improve their financial situation. Remember that in this economy, everyone is interested in getting themselves into a better financial position.

Financial concerns are at the top of everyone's mind because of all the things that have happened fiscally over the past few years. The poor performance of the stock market, the real estate market, the banking system, and many other key industries have had a major negative impact on everyone's financial results and success.

Unemployment is high, companies continue to downsize, and new jobs are not being created fast enough, creating an increased level of financial fear for everyone.

These concerns, however, have a positive benefit for raising private money. That financial fear, uncertainty, and doubt has pushed most people down to the lowest survival level, according to Maslow's Hierarchy of Needs.

This means that everyone is looking for ways to enhance, change, or create a better financial position for themselves, their families, and their businesses. They are also considering other investment asset classes to add to their portfolios and are open to understanding new investment prospects.

This financial environment and financial fear mindset provides a great opportunity for the private money raiser, because it ensures that a lot more people are seeking innovative investment opportunities to grow their financial portfolios.

Many people have had their financial resources reduced or eliminated as a result of the negative turmoil in our economy, the market, and their investments. Very few people focus on self-actualization, which is at the very top of Maslow's Hierarchy of Needs.

It is safe to assume that everyone you meet is worrying about how to get out of their financial hole and how to build the financial resources they need and want. Many wonder if they will ever get enough money to retire and to live the lifestyle they want. In fact, data shows that many people are postponing retirement because they simply can't afford it.

You should discard the belief that people are not interested in the topic because they are absolutely interested in building more financial security for themselves and their families.

The real question is, can you build trust with them and demonstrate that you have the capabilities to help them achieve their financial goals? Can you help them change their financial situation and fiscal condition? Can you help them get to where they want to go?

You cannot help them until you have built a trusting, caring relationship and you understand where they are trying to go. This is just one more reason why a telling-and-selling approach will backfire on you every time because people need to know that you care about them and what they are striving to achieve before they start to trust you enough to listen to what you have to say.

This is great news for the person who is serious about raising private money and someone who can filter out their internal mind chatter, that voice in their head that keeps saying, "I don't think they need me or my services to help them build or rebuild their financial resources."

Having a high level of personal effectiveness allows you to develop an action plan and then hold yourself accountable to take those actions. A high level of effectiveness will allow you to take new actions every week and ensure you're making progress toward achieving your goal.

One of the biggest reasons people report a lack of progress toward their private money goal is a shortage of time. Using time as an excuse for not taking enough actions reveals that the real issue is *not* time. The real reason is that raising private money is not a high-enough priority for them, and therefore, they didn't schedule enough time for implementing the actions required to achieve success. Alternately, they are procrastinating because they do not want to engage in conversation with private money sources about what they do because they perceive it to be a very fearful situation.

To be more effective at raising private money, you must master the ability to overcome procrastination. Poor time management and chronic procrastination are the top two reasons why people don't achieve their goals. Some would say that poor time management and chronic procrastination are at the very heart of Personal Effectiveness failure, and I would tend to agree with them. If you want to significantly increase your success at raising private money, address your poor time management and chronic procrastination. You will be pleasantly surprised at the increase in private money that results from this simple change in your behavior.

To really master Personal Effectiveness, you must have clear goals and an action plan, and allocate sufficient time to complete your activities. Successful individuals make time for private money rather than waiting until they have time.

To achieve greater success at raising private money, you must stop yourself from procrastinating. Continuing to procrastinate makes it easier to ignore activities week after week. If you do so and repeatedly delay taking action, at some point the year will be over, and you will have missed your private money goals.

Becoming more effective requires a commitment from you to keep working at implementing personal effectiveness best practices each day, each week, and each month. It is only through taking committed action to improve your personal effectiveness that you will transform your results with raising private money from where they are today to where you want them to be.

This information may feel like a review of the basic personal effective information you think you know. In your mind, you are probably saying to yourself, "I know this information already." Yes, I know you understand the best practices for being more personally effective. At least you know them conceptually.

But the real question is, to what degree are you implementing the best practices for being more personally effective, and how consistently are you using them in regard to raising private money?

To be very clear, the Inner Game challenge of being more Personally Effective is that what you know does not help your performance or increase your results because it is not what you know about being more personally effective that produces greater private money results. It is, however, how much of what you know that you're consistently implementing that creates greater success.

It's easy for you to stop implementing what your mind would say are basic, personal effectiveness practices. That is, however, a recipe for private money failure.

In the world of sports, when a team talks about "getting back to basics," you know that they have lost their way and have just experienced their worst season.

On the other hand, winners never stop doing the basics because they know they are the keys to consistent success. In fact, they have processes and measurements to ensure they are always implementing the basics at a very high completion level.

The magic Reflective Assessment Questions are:
1. How consistently are you implementing the personal effectiveness best practices for raising private money?
2. Do you even know how consistently you're implementing the best practices for raising private money?
3. Do you need to get back to implementing the personal effective best practices for raising private money?

Personal Effectiveness Assessment

Use the following assessment tool to understand your level of personal effectiveness for raising private money, by answering the questions and then rating yourself. Use the blank rows at the bottom of the document to add any Personal Effectiveness best practices that are missing for you.

Make sure that you modify this tool to make it your own. This should only take a few minutes; use it regularly to increase your personal effectiveness so that you will enhance your private money success.

Raising Private Money Personal Effectiveness Assessment

Assessment Questions	Rating				
	1	2	3	4	5
Do you have clear, documented private money goals: weekly, monthly, quarterly, and annually?					
Do you have a detailed, documented action plan including the steps necessary to achieve your private money goals?					
Are you scheduling time for private money activities into your calendar?					
Have you made a commitment to a specific number of hours and number of private money conversations you are going to accomplish each week?					
Are you holding yourself accountable for taking daily and weekly private money-raising actions?					
Are you measuring and tracking your completion ratios for your private money commitments versus the actual results?					
Are you addressing any procrastination issues as they arise?					
Are you practicing your private money scripts daily?					
Are you role-playing your private money conversations daily with different partners?					
Are you making weekly and monthly commitments to your private money performance coach?					
Are you using a private money support buddy weekly to help you stay accountable and on track for achieving your private money goals?					

Are you modifying and updating your action plan as you learn what works and what doesn't?					
Are you talking to potential private money sources daily and weekly?					
Totals					
Rating Total #		/ 15 x 5	Total Number/Items #	Effectiveness Percentage percent	

Take a moment to answer the following questions about this exercise.

    a. What insights did you gain, if any, from the exercise?

    b. Based on those insights, what actions are you going to take that will increase the amount of private money you will raise over the next six months? Schedule the actions into your organizer or planner.

    c. Complete the actions on time without any delays or procrastinations.

In the next chapter, you will learn how your self-image is blocking you from raising more private money. You will also discover how your self-image prevents you from using the effective private money raising practices you have learned.

Chapter Three

SELF-IMAGE PSYCHOLOGY

THE NEXT IMPORTANT COMPONENT OF the Inner Game of raising private money is Self-Image Psychology, sometimes referred to as Performance Psychology.

Self-Image Psychology focuses on your thoughts, feelings, and emotions about raising private money and your private money sources. It also deals with the reoccurring thoughts, feelings, and emotions that you have when you are engaged in a private money conversation.

Your thoughts, feelings, and emotions about all aspects of raising private money will impact the results that you get. Because it governs your performance, Self-Image Psychology is a critical component of your Inner Game.

Do your conversations with potential sources leave you feeling like they don't trust you? Remember, the internal negative thoughts and feelings will impact your private money performance. If you have a negative attitude about raising private money, it will negatively impact your performance. If your attitude is that people will not want to talk with you about private money or that they will not see you as someone with a solution that will help them rebuild their financial resources, that attitude will also negatively impact your performance and results.

A good way to understand attitude is to think of it as an airplane. In an airplane, attitude is the direction that it leans. So to understand your attitude about raising private money, simply ask yourself in which direction do you lean? If you lean toward raising private money with private money conversations, you have a positive attitude toward it. If you lean away from raising private money and those conversations, you have a negative attitude about it.

That negative attitude will keep you avoiding and keep you from completing raising private money activities. Many times this avoidant behavior will be unconscious, and you won't even notice that you keep finding creative reasons and wonderful excuses not to follow through with your commitments.

To achieve greater success, you must adjust your attitude so that you lean toward completing private money-raising activities. Also with the right attitude, you will enthusiastically, and without hesitation, engage in raising private money conversations with the people you meet.

Your beliefs will impact your private money performance and results. As such, it is important that you know what your underlining beliefs are in regard to raising private money. To understand your beliefs, take a few moments to answer the following reflective assessment questions:

1. Is it your belief that people won't trust you?
2. Is it your belief that you have to "tell and sell" in your conversations to achieve your private money goals?
3. Is it your belief that people don't have money?
4. Is it your belief that you don't know anyone with money to invest?
5. Is it your belief that a busy professional or high net worth individual won't talk to you?
6. Is it your belief that networking to raise private money will not work?
7. Is it your belief that developing and cultivating long-term relationships are not effective for raising private money?
8. Please list below five of your limiting beliefs that may be blocking your effectiveness in regard to raising private money:

_____

_____

Realize that these limiting beliefs are all self-imposed, created within your mind, your Inner Game. They're a part of your current Self-Image Psychology in regard to raising private money. These negative—and untrue—beliefs will impact your ability to raise all the private money you need, want, and desire.

To be more effective, you must align your beliefs to ones that will support you in raising private money; otherwise, you will not take the actions necessary to achieve your private money goals. Aligning your beliefs to your goals is the way to unlock your full potential so that you can engage effectively with your private money sources.

Can you change your beliefs, so they are in alignment with your goals for raising private money? If you are unable, or unwilling, to change your beliefs, you won't implement the winning strategies and best practices for raising private money that you've learned. Implementation is the key to effectiveness and achieving greater results. The truth is, you can't achieve results from winning strategies and best practices that you are not implementing.

In addition to beliefs, expectations play a major role in your private money effectiveness and financial success. What do you expect when you are talking with a potential private money source?

1. Do you expect the person to trust you?
2. Do you expect the person to be truly interested in what you have to say?
3. Do you expect to schedule a follow-up meeting to speak together again?
4. Do you expect to achieve your monthly private money goal?
5. Do you expect that raising private money will be easy or hard?
6. Do you expect your private money source will feel your excitement and enthusiasm?
7. Do you expect to develop a long-term relationship with the private money source?
8. Do you expect that the private money source will commit to a deal right away?
9. Please list below five of your limiting expectations that may be blocking your effectiveness in regard to raising private money:

It has been proven that you tend to get what you really expect in life, as well as in raising private money. Changing your expectations will change your performance and your results. Therefore, when you increase your expectation with regard to the amount of private money you will raise, it will, in fact, result in a significant increase in the amount of money you actually raise.

Your expectations have a huge impact on your performance and your life. More and more people are learning that you achieve in life what you truly expect to, not what you want or what you hope for.

Take a look at the level of private money you are currently raising. If you just change your expectation for that amount, you would raise more. Whatever amount of private money you are raising right now, that level is within your comfort zone. The term *comfort zone* is just another way to describe your current expectations.

For example, if you are consistently raising $20,000 from your private money sources, that is your current private money comfort zone. Whatever amount of money you are consistently raising is matching your real expectation. So the actions that you are currently taking always matches the amount of money that you feel is within your comfort zone; otherwise, you would be driven to take different actions.

There is one more self-imposed barrier to be pointed out that limits the use of your potential. This item is: *excuses*. What are the excuses that you believe to be true and that you keep making to yourself about why you're not raising more private money? The excuses that you accept as the truth are the real reasons for your current level of success or lack thereof. But these excuses are false, and they don't have to limit your private money-raising performance or the results you achieve.

Think of it this way. As you continue raising private money, your excuses will stop you from taking action and will stop you from giving your all to achieve your goals. Below are a few of the

most common excuses people buy into that block their private money-raising effectiveness, performance and their results:
1. I'm just too busy to follow up.
2. I don't have the time.
3. I'm not sure that they have money.
4. I don't think they trust me.
5. There must be an easier way.
6. I don't know anyone with private money to invest.
7. I don't know enough yet about raising private money.
8. I need to practice my scripts more.
9. I don't think I should go to the networking event tonight because _____ (*fill in the blank*).
10. I didn't do it because _____ (*fill in the blank*).

Here is a great exercise to discover what excuses you're allowing that are stopping you from raising more private money. Take a moment and recall the amount of private money that you have raised over the past few months. For example, let's say that you have raised $100,000 of private money in the last six months.

With that number in mind or the number that is relevant and appropriate for your situation, answer the following questions:
1. Why haven't you raised twice that amount?
   - Why not $200,000?
2. Why haven't you raised 10 times that amount?
   - Why not $1,000,000?
3. If you haven't raised any private money during the last six months, why not?

You may have answered with reasons (excuses) like the ones listed below:
1. I don't know any busy professionals or high net worth people.
2. I don't know anyone who has money.
3. I don't have a private money-raising track record, so why would anyone trust me?
4. I'm too busy.
5. I don't have the time.
6. I haven't closed a deal yet.

Self-Image Psychology

7. I'm not sure exactly what to say to someone.
8. I'm afraid of losing their money.
9. I don't know enough yet.
10. People keep telling me no.
11. I don't get a positive response from the people I talk to.

All of these answers may sound like great reasons for not raising more private money, and many of them may even be true. You may not have closed a deal yet, or you may be afraid of losing someone's money. However, none of these are the real reason you haven't raised more private money. They are excuses you use to justify the lack of actions you're taking necessary to raise a much higher amount of private money than you have so far.

Your reasons or excuses make you feel comfortable with your current level of results, but they are not a reflection of your full potential for raising private money. Why? Because you have the potential to find private money sources and to engage them in an effective private money conversation that lead to success. You possess the potential to overcome your fear of losing people's money.

You already have the potential to raise millions in private money, but you won't commit yourself completely to make that happen if you continue to allow your reasons and excuses to stop you from taking consistent action. You must become aware of the fact that your reasons and excuses are false before you can achieve greater private money-raising results. Your reasons and excuses are a product of your Self-Image Psychology, your performance psychology, that internal game going on inside your mind in regard to raising private money.

How do you know that your reasons and excuses are false? Here's how. If there is anyone else that has the same conditions and in a similar situation to yours in regard to raising private money, but they are achieving success in raising private money, then your reasons or excuses are false. If someone else with your exact issues achieved success in raising private money, then so can you.

If they are in the same situation as you, but they overcame the challenges and the barriers to achieving success—you can, too.

I am part of a wonderful community of private money raisers and in that community:
1. We have had people who have never completed an investment opportunity before continuing on to raise millions in private money.
2. We have had people who were afraid of losing someone's money continue on to raise millions in private money.
3. We have had people who did not know any busy professionals or high net worth individuals continue on to raise millions in private money.
4. We have had people who were not sure of what to say continue on to raise millions in private money.
5. We have had people who did not have time continue on to raise millions in private money.

Regardless of the reason or excuse that you declare, there is someone in the community with that exact issue, who overcame it and continued on to become a successful, private money superstar.

Don't let any reasons or excuses determine how much of your private money potential you use. Don't let yourself off the hook for not taking sufficient action to achieve your goals. Others with the same issues have found ways to achieve success. So can you, but you must first stop accepting any reasons or excuses as the true predictor of your abilities.

Take a moment and write down any aha's or insights that you've received from reading this chapter and answering the assessment questions. Add to your calendar or organizer any actions you're going to take as a result of reading this chapter and then follow through by completing the recorded actions.

We'll discuss how to align, modify, or change your attitude, beliefs, expectations, and excuse-making to support you in achieving your private money goals in an upcoming chapter.

Chapter Four

THE POWER OF BELIEFS

YOUR BELIEFS ARE SO STRONG that they shape how you act, how you behave, and most importantly, the results you achieve.

How you define something, such as raising private money, comes out of your belief system.

For example, what is your belief about what you are trying to accomplish when you are talking to a private money source? If you believe the purpose of the conversation is about telling, selling, and overcoming objections, that belief will impact your behavior, which will definitely influence how you conduct the conversation.

If your belief is that you are there to sell them on private lending, you will find yourself describing a deal and selling the benefits of private lending. Because of your beliefs, you would treat their questions as objections. Instead of engaging them in a discussion to understand their situation, you would use more telling and selling to overcome their perceived objections, and you wouldn't ever answer their questions directly or to their satisfaction.

That whole approach to your private money conversations is doomed because of your belief about why you are having the discussion in the first place. If you believe you should be telling, selling, and overcoming objections, then you have the belief structure of a salesperson. Armed with this belief, you would act and talk like a salesperson on a sales call, because telling, selling, and overcoming objections is the standard approach to closing the sale. It is a very me-centered approach to a conversation, and it is not very engaging.

On the other hand, consider defining your conversations with private money sources not as selling situations, but rather as opportunities for engaging in dialogs of understanding and trust-building conversations that provide real value. Your goal is to understand what they are striving to achieve and to explore just how you might help them achieve that goal. You are now a problem solver, helping them address a pressing problem that they really want to resolve.

This change in belief about why you are engaging with a private money source will alter your entire approach. You will find yourself truly concerned and caring for them. Because you're striving to understand their personal situation, you'll ask appealing questions that will allow you to build both trust and rapport very quickly.

Your every action, the words that you use, the questions you ask, your body language, and your whole being will demonstrate to your potential private money source that you are interested in them and how to help them. These behaviors will create the environment necessary for creating an effective conversation—one that enhances your relationship.

What if you believed that the purpose of a conversation with your private money source was to create a long-term relationship? That the purpose of the meeting was not to walk out of the meeting with them wanting to participate in your deal? Instead, you believed that you were there to develop a new relationship, to begin building trust and credibility, and to share your excitement and that you were there to understand their situation, their goals, and what they are trying to accomplish both financially and in regard to living their desired lifestyle.

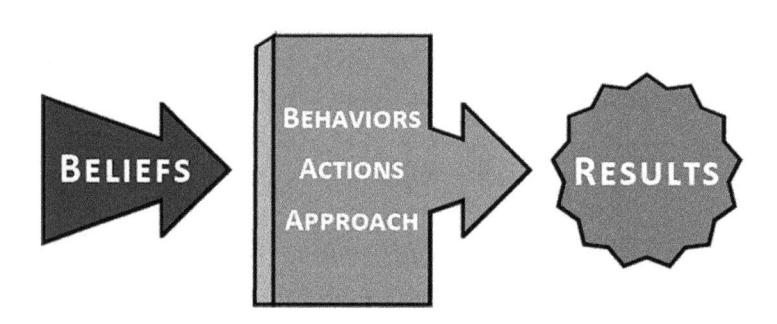

BELIEFS → **BEHAVIORS ACTIONS APPROACH** → **RESULTS**

Undoubtedly how you define something determines how you relate to it and your approach to accomplishing it. The same is true for raising private money. How you define the purpose of your private money conversation will determine your approach for engaging with your private money sources, significantly impacting your results.

If you believe that you are talking with your private money sources to get them to loan you money, or you are there begging for money, you will act and behave very differently than if you felt your reason for being there was to understand their situations and their goals. You would find yourself being much more interested *in* them, instead of working hard on being interesting *to* them.

This shift in your beliefs will produce very different and very beneficial results for building the relationship and for you. Your behaviors will also be different because of how you define your purpose for engaging with a private money source.

The following are some critical reflective assessment questions to answer before you engage with a potential private money source:
1. What is your purpose in having the conversation?
2. What are you trying to accomplish?
3. How do you define the relationship at that moment in time?
4. What is your primary reason for engaging with them?

When you change the purpose for having a conversation with your private money sources to one that is focused on understanding their goals and to generate excitement within them, the dynamics of your conversation will change for the positive very quickly.

Here is a great teaching example. In talking to a Private Money Raiser I know, he told me that he didn't understand why the people he was talking to didn't jump quickly into his deals. He complained, "I'm offering them more money than what they can get from a bank or any other investment institution and a greater return than what they're getting on their current investments. In some cases, I'm offering them a great interest rate and part of the profit. I don't understand why they can't see the great opportunities I'm giving them."

As the Private Money Raiser continued to drone on about all the things he was offering, I finally said

Enough! You've been talking for five minutes about all the things that you would do for your private money source. You describe the features and benefits for them, but I haven't heard you say one time that you understand what *they* are trying to achieve. I have not heard you describe a single question that you asked them to understand their situation, so it is highly unlikely you are engaging in any sort of conversation with them. Instead, you're "telling and selling," not building trust or credibility with them.

In addition, I have not heard anything in your tone, your body language, or in your presentation that lets me know you established rapport, built trust, or even that you care about your private money source at all. All I heard is what you want and how their life would be so much better if they only did what you want. It would be very difficult for anyone to believe you care about them or to trust you, given your approach, because you're not asking any questions to help you understand them and their needs. At this point in the relationship, you haven't earned the right to even be considered as a credible person let alone an investment source.

You assume that if you wave around a higher rate of interest than what they are currently getting, along with a promise of some of the backend profits, that they'll go down on their knees begging to be your private money source. The reality is that your private money source is experiencing you as someone with a very 'me' centered conversation.

To be clear, your private money source doesn't really care about what you want, nor do they want to hear what you're offering until they know that you care about them. They want some indication that you are genuinely interested in helping them achieve their goals and that you care about their concerns before they even hear you, let alone entertain your offer.

The approach of trying to convince someone of obtaining a significant higher return and backend profits may have the very opposite effect than you intended. It may raise concerns because you are telling and selling and not engaging in a conversation that builds rapport and trust.

If you continue this approach, your potential private money sources will see you simply as a salesperson with a pitch, someone who doesn't understand their needs or care about them. They will perceive you as self-absorbed. Is this really what you want when you are seeking to build effective, long-term relationships with potential private money sources?

If you think that you're engaging in a private money conversation to present the person a higher interest rate before you have established a proper relationship, it will be reflected in your approach. The consequences of that action will produce less than desired results.

This approach is not a winning strategy or best practice for raising private money. Investment institutions use this approach: "Invest with us and you will receive a higher return." Unfortunately, this message frequently has failed to meet investors' expectations of higher returns promised by investment institutions.

Today, people are looking for someone that they trust, someone who cares about them, someone who they have a relationship with, and someone who understands what they are trying to achieve. This is the strategy that will be effective in raising private money. Best practices for raising private money include asking good questions, generating excitement, demonstrating your credibility, building affinity and trust, listening eighty percent of the time while talking only twenty percent of the time, and always taking a long-term view of the relationship. Being genuinely interested in them is probably the most important best practice you can use.

Remember, you are not there to sell them something that they do not need or want. Here are just a few things you should know about your potential private money sources:

1. What is their name?
2. Do they have a family, friends? Who are they and what do they do?
3. Where do they live? How long have they lived there?
4. Where do they work? What do they like about their profession?
5. Are they interested in sports? What is their favorite team?
6. What are their hobbies?
7. What do they do for entertainment and relaxation?
8. What are they trying to accomplish?
9. What are their concerns?
10. What are they trying to accomplish financially?
    a. You don't start with this question. You can only ask this question after you have built rapport and established a level of trust.
11. What are their financial concerns?
    a. Once again you don't start with this question. You can only ask this question after you have built rapport and established a level of trust.

These are just a few questions to help you engage in a conversation with a potential private money source that will create a great foundation for building rapport, trust, and a long-term relationship.

Here's an example of a conversation that occurred during a flight across the country. During the flight, I started up a conversation with a couple seated next to me. Throughout the course of the conversation, I learned about their family and their favorite sports team. They shared with me that they had been hit pretty hard financially when the market dropped and the housing market collapsed. As a result, they have some real concerns that they will not be able to pay for the college education of their three children. Their children, are close to each other in age; therefore, they will be in college around the same time. They indicated that they have done a great job of saving some money in a college fund, but they don't see how they will be able to have enough money by the time it's needed.

Analyze this example carefully. Their primary concern is not how to get a higher interest rate or higher return on investments. Instead, their primary concern is where they will get the funds needed to put their three kids through college. Talking to them about a higher interest rate would not have piqued their interest, but engaging them in a conversation about their primary concern (how to pay for their children's college education) will definitely get their attention.

The key point here is there was no mention of private lending or private money until they asked me what I did. By that time, I had built rapport, trust, and a foundation for building a longer-term relationship. I had also gathered a great amount of information about them, their priorities, their concerns, and their situation. The next step was not to go into a telling-and-selling mode about private lending or private money but to deliver my story and pique their interest.

> I worked as an engineer in corporate America for over fifteen years, and I always did well for myself. I got to an age where I wanted to start making sure I could replace my income with other income so that I could maintain my lifestyle as I approached retirement.
>
> So I spoke to some of the top financial advisors out there and was given all the Wall Street income-producing vehicles such as bonds, dividend paying stocks, and so forth. Here's what I found out. Bonds, dividends, stocks, and other Wall Street income-producing vehicles didn't keep up with inflation. I was losing my buying power, and what was worse was that I wasn't positioning myself for retirement.
>
> Then I looked at alternative investments such as real estate, and I purchased some income-producing properties. And then I discovered that when compared with

three important factors, which are liquidity, returns, and risk, there is another vehicle that beats owning income property hands down in terms of producing income. I realized quickly that I'm either taking too much risk, or I would have to live well below my current standard of living.

Then I discovered private lending. Here's why I love it.

I found it's relatively safe compared to other investment vehicles when it comes to consistent monthly income. I learned that it explains why banks are everywhere and that the bank's business model is a great one. In terms of liquidity, returns, and risk, the banking model beats income properties hands down.

I'm a very skeptical person, and so my first thought was, what would happen if the borrower stopped paying me? It turns out that the money is backed by real estate with companies out there specializing in handling all that. In fact, if a borrower doesn't pay, I get their property. Just like any bank would.

Then I thought, why isn't everybody doing this? I realized that the wealthiest people actually do participate in lending like this. It is a game they have been playing for a very long time. Today, private lending is my main focus, and I see hopes of maintaining my current standard of living because of it. It blows my mind that people don't realize this is one of the safer ways to generate income. I have doctors, attorneys, and engineers involved with me now.

And now, some of my family and friends have asked to participate with me, so I let them. I'm helping them generate the income they need to support them in creating their own desired lifestyles.

Then I returned to my approach of engaging them in a conversation about them. I was perfectly fine with getting off the plane knowing that I had established the foundation for a positive follow-up conversation with them, based on the relationship we built. The successful strategy was not to tell and sell and overcome objections, but rather to engage people in trust-building and excitement-building conversations. There are two people who we can learn a lot from in this regard. The first is conversationalist, Larry King.

Larry King has had a very successful talk show for many years. His key to success was not only to have the right people on the show, but also to engage them in conversation through asking information-eliciting questions. If you watch him, you will notice that he only talks about twenty percent of the time—or less—while listening the remaining eighty to ninety percent of the time. He's a master at asking engrossing questions and then waiting for the person to respond. He doesn't rush them or try to steer them in any particular direction. He just asks good questions, waits for the answer, continually connecting with them.

As a result of this style, Larry's guests share information about themselves, and many times share information that they may not have shared in any other interviews. Why does this happen? It's because he's interested in his guests, it's because of the level of trust he creates with them, and it's because of the way he treats them. As a result, many guests are eager to reappear on his show. He is truly a master at engaging with others.

Notice that he doesn't expect anything from his guests other than to have an engaging conversation with them. He makes sure they are the focus and the center of the discussion. At no time is he telling or selling, but he is always asking interesting questions, building trust, and enhancing the relationship with his guest.

The second person to watch and study is Oprah Winfrey, another master at engaging people in a conversation in which she creates rapport, builds trust, and establishes a base for a long-term relationship. If you watch Oprah, you will see her connect with her guests on such an intimate level that you experience what they feel. She is totally focused on listening and hearing what they have to say.

As you watch her, pay close attention to what she does to make the person feel special, cared for, and appreciated. Notice her body language. She is communicating that she is there to hear what you have to say. It appears that she is learning something from every guest she interviews. Quite often throughout her conversations, you will hear her repeat something that the person said and grab her notebook and say, "I've got to write this down; this is so good."

If you asked Oprah why she was having the conversation, she would say her goal is to be authentic, to build trust, to develop a relationship, and to truly understand the other person's point of view and situation. It is all about them, connecting with them on a much deeper level than you could ever achieve through a telling-and-selling approach.

Larry King and Oprah Winfrey are just two people who do a fabulous job of engaging people in effective conversations by asking questions, building trust, and developing a foundation for a long-term relationship. They also obtain a significant amount of information about their guest, their situation, and their priorities.

Neither Larry King nor Oprah Winfrey are interested in telling and selling their guest on anything. Anyone can obviously see that they are engaging for the purpose of hearing their guest's story. They ask effective questions, listening intently more than eighty percent of the time. They're not trying to impress their guests. They're very confident in their ability to have an honest conversation.

As you watch them, you will see that their interviews are much more like conversations instead of interrogations. The quality of their discussions are very much like that of two old friends talking over a cup of coffee rather than someone trying to impress the other.

Just as with Larry King and Oprah Winfrey, there is a huge advantage when you can engage your private money sources for the purpose of understanding them, their goals, and their situations without being concerned about pushing your own agenda.

Before engaging in any conversation, you will need to define the purpose of meeting with potential private money sources. How you define your purpose will determine your approach. It will also determine how effective you will be at raising private money.

Take a moment and define the purpose of having a conversation with a potential or existing private money source. Here are some reflective assessment questions that will help define your purpose or reason for the conversation:
1. What is your purpose when talking to a potential private money source?
2. What are you trying to accomplish through the conversation?
3. How do you define the relationship with your private money source at that moment in time?
4. What is your primary reason for talking with them?
5. Develop your purpose statement for having a private money conversation. This statement helps you create a new belief in regard to why you engage in conversations with your private money sources. It will also support you in aligning your behaviors to the new belief.

Example of a purpose statement:

> My purpose is to help my private money sources achieve the goals and desires that they want. I seek to understand their concerns and then support them in finding ways to resolve or eliminate the challenge. I am a problem solver, supporting my private money sources in solving issues that are blocking them from having the financial resources they need to live the lifestyle that they desire.
>
> I do not use a telling-and-selling approach to force my will onto my private money source. Instead, I engage them in conversation where I am listening for the purpose of understanding what they are truly trying to achieve. From my understanding of their goals and concerns, if I have valuable information to share with them, I do.

> I am deeply committed to sharing financial information and financial education so that my private money sources can make informed financial choices."

You can create your own purpose statement, one that is reflective of the intention you want to have when you engage with your private money sources. Remember that how you define raising private money will determine how you relate to it, your approach for raising private money and your results. Consider and make your choice wisely, selecting a definition that reflects the richer service you will provide to your private money partners.

Post copies of your finished purpose statement where you can read it often, and make sure that you read it just before you engage in conversation with your private money sources. This practice of reading your statement will help you align your behaviors with the intentions embodied in your statement.

In the next chapter, you will discover what external support you require to help you implement the winning strategies and best practices for raising more private money. You only achieve accelerated results and success from the actions you are taking and not from what you know.

You will also discover what support you need to overcome both the Inner and Outer Game challenges you will encounter on your journey to increasing the amount of money you raise by ten times.

Chapter Five

MILLION DOLLAR SUPPORT PROGRAM

SUCCESSFUL PEOPLE, AND SUCCESSFUL PRIVATE Money Raisers, will tell you that you need support from experts to truly achieve accelerated results.

It is impossible for you to have all the knowledge, skills, and expertise (Outer Game) that you require to take raising private money to the next level. More than likely you don't know all the winning strategies and **SUPPORT PROGRAM** best practices for raising private money because these strategies and practices are always changing. That is why it is important to have a support team of Outer Game experts because they will have specialized knowledge in the area you require help.

It is also very important to hire an Inner Game coach to help you achieve breakthrough results with private money and to support you in continuing to increase the amount of money you raise. For example, you set a goal to raise $200,000 in private money, and you start achieving that amount consistently. What happens in this situation is that your mindset locks on to the $200,000, and that amount becomes who you see yourself to be, someone who can raise that amount of money but not necessarily more. The $200,000 becomes your new private money comfort zone, but it does not reflect the full use of your potential to raise greater amounts of money.

To be clear, whatever amount of private money you are currently raising is consistent with your current comfort zone. That amount

The Inner Game of Raising Private Money

is, in fact, who you see yourself to be. Therefore, it is impossible to have a significant increase in the amount of money you raise without addressing your Inner Game challenges.

Research shows that it is very difficult if not impossible to identify and resolve your own Inner Game challenges without outside help. This is so because your Inner Game challenges are so much a part of who you think you are that you can't even see how these challenges are blocking your success.

In the example above, a Raising Private Money Inner Game coach and a support team of private money-raising experts will help you continually increase the amount of money you raise and accelerate your progress toward financial success.

Working with your Inner Game Coach, you can move from raising $200,000 to $400,000, and from $400,000 to $1,000,000 and even beyond. There is truly no limit to the amount of private money you can raise if you have the right Inner Game Coach and experts supporting you in a programmatic way.

Being supported by a well-rounded private money-raising program, one that is designed specifically to ensure that you are consistently implementing the winning strategies and best practices, overcoming inner Game challenges, and making progress toward your private money goals, is essential for accelerating and sustaining your success.

A raising private money implementation program with this type of support has proven to be worth millions of dollars to the private money raisers who have been fortunate enough to participate in it. The name, Million Dollar Support Program, is based on the many suggestions from the programs' participants, testifying to the great success they achieved as a result of the program.

> The Inner Game Coach I had on my team from the Million Dollar Program helped me to raise millions of dollars of private money. Every week my coach made sure that I implemented the best practices for raising private money, and gave me real-time tips and techniques that worked great. His support allowed me to quickly beat any challenges or blocks that I faced, and he kept me moving forward, ultimately exceeding my private money goals.
>
> ~ Aaron ~

Million Dollar Support Program

In discussion with many of the program participants, one of the reoccurring themes was "this program is worth a million dollars." Therefore, the name Million Dollar became a driving force for the value and the benefit we strived to deliver for each participant.

It is clear that achieving private money success is much easier when you are part of a high-quality implementation program with an Inner Game Coach and a team of Outer Game private money-raising experts supporting you. When you think about it, what entertainer, athlete, sports team, or entrepreneur does *not* have a team of experts supporting them in implementing winning strategies and best practices? Who helps them overcome both Inner Game and Outer Game challenges? You don't have to look too hard before you find that implementation support is a standard practice for anyone committed to achieving success and sustaining it. It is safe to say that if you are serious about increasing the amount of private money you raise and accelerating your private money results, you must use experts to support you in a programmatic way.

Reasons to Hire a Private Money-Raising Coach and Their Support Team.

Here are the major reasons people serious about raising more private money hire an implementation coach and a support team of experts to help them raise more private money:

1. To help me become effective at raising private money.
2. To teach me the winning strategies and best practices for becoming a private money magnet.
3. To help me create an overarching plan for my private money business, based on the winning strategies and best practices for raising private money.
4. To help me build an implementation plan that allows me to achieve my private money goals faster and easier.
5. To hold me accountable for implementing my plan, taking private money actions, and achieving results.
6. To challenge and push me so that I stretch beyond my current comfort Zone for raising private money.

7. To listen and to hear me without judgment or criticism in order to support me in getting out of my own way.
8. To help me overcome nonproductive habits so that I consistently achieve my private money goals.
9. To provide me with ongoing encouragement and support.
10. To provide me with unbiased and objective feedback.
11. To keep me on track and moving forward toward my goal even when I encounter setbacks.
12. To ensure that I ultimately achieve my private money goals.
13. To connect me to the right experts and support resources so that I achieve private money success faster.

Private money raisers that have fully utilized an implementation program that included the support discussed here were able to raise more money than they could use. Many of them had to expand their business model to use the additional private money they had raised, amounts far beyond their expectations *and* their imagination.

Where the Million Dollar Support Program is Different than a Standard or a Generic Coaching Program

It is different from other coaching programs because at the very heart of the program is an Inner Game coach who is a master at helping you overcome your Inner Game challenges so that you unlock your private money-raising potential and achieve accelerated results.

The Million Dollar Support Program also has private money-raising expertise, knowledge, experience, and a deep mastery of what it takes to support you in implementing the best practices of raising private money to achieve outstanding financial results. It offers much more than generic coaching because it provides breakthrough coaching and consulting from experienced experts in raising private money.

There is nothing wrong with a general coach or with most generic coaching programs. However, generic coaching programs have a different goal and a different approach than the Million Dollar Support Program. The Million Dollar Support Program is specifically designed to help you raise more private money and to support you in achieving a ten-time increase in the amount of money that you raise.

Let me say a little more about the difference between the two types of programs. A generic coach is at the heart of most coaching programs. They are trained to ask questions. A very good coach can help you achieve outstanding results from asking empowering questions, but a generic or a standard coach doesn't understand the winning strategies and best practices for raising private money.

They don't have the special expertise, the knowledge, or experience to help you overcome the Inner Game and Outer Game challenges unique to raising private money that you will encounter. A standard coach's questioning approach will work—if you have all the skills and capabilities you need, if you have all the answers inside of you, and if you have all the time in the world to research the answers you require to be successful and to develop the skills required on your own before you take action.

Because the Million Dollar Support Program has Inner Game masters and experts on the team who know the winning strategies and best practices for raising private money, they are able to help you develop a better plan of action—a plan specifically designed to help you raise more private money faster and with less effort. Also, because these experts have expertise and experience in raising private money, they are able to provide real-time support for those unique challenges that you encounter as you move toward raising all the money you need. Additionally, the program experts will help you develop the skills and abilities required to raise more money faster.

Hopefully, you can see that a program specifically designed for raising private money, with an Inner Game Master and with raising private money Outer Game experts to support you in achieving breakthrough performance as a critical part of that design, will produce superior results in a more accelerated period of time.

Because you are already clear that you want to become better at raising private money, a program focused on helping you achieve that goal is much more valuable. If you are not clear that raising private money is your focus and your goal, then generic coaching or life coaching may be the more appropriate approach to help you figure out what you really wanted.

A Million Dollar Support Program Example

The following is an example of what my Million Dollar Support Program is designed to do in helping you raise unlimited amounts of private money to support your business and financial goals.

You enter into the Million Dollar Support Program only after you have successfully completed a workshop, seminar, training event, or some educational program on raising private money. Therefore, you have already been trained on the winning strategies and best practices, and your goal and objective is to use the knowledge to raise higher levels of private money and to go beyond the level of success that you had in the past, or that you could achieve without an effective support program.

You are assigned an implementation expert who understands the winning strategies and best practices for raising private money. This expert is an Inner Game coach who becomes your primary contact and interface throughout your participation in the program. Yes, you will interface with other experts on your support team, but there will be one person responsible for tracking your actions and progress as you implement the program until, ultimately, you achieve your private money goals.

This person is your personal private money-raising implementation expert. He or she will be accountable to make sure you have every opportunity to be successful; and that nothing, in regard to you or your progress, is dropped or slips through the cracks.

The Million Dollar Support Coach initial goal is to establish an effective working relationship with you, by understanding your operating style and what ways of working together is most effective for you. These implementation experts know that one style doesn't fit everyone. They strive to tailor their styles and their approaches to have positive impacts on the outcomes you produce. If, for some reason, you or your assigned coach feels that he or she is not the right implementation expert for you, he/she will discuss the issue with you and then, if agreed, reassign you to a different coach — one that is more compatible with your operating style.

Million Dollar Support Program

The overriding objective of the Million Dollar Support coach is to ensure that you have the right support plan in place to produce maximum results in support of your goals.

You and your Million Dollar Support coach will discuss and then agree on an engagement schedule. You may want to engage with your coach every week, every two weeks, or once a month. The frequency should fit with your working style, your workload, and your support requirements. Some clients feel that engaging every week is too much, as it does not provide them with enough time between sessions to implement the actions they have committed to complete. Others want the internal pressure created from engaging with their coaches every other week. Some prefer not to deal with the higher levels of stress that come from weekly commitments and agree on meeting monthly or bi-monthly. The program is designed to fit your needs, preferences, and style.

The frequency with which you meet with your coach is your decision, since we know the best programs are created to meet and exceed your specific needs. Should you begin with an agreed frequency schedule and desire a change, simply address the matter with your coach to arrange a new schedule that better suits your needs. Once the frequency is determined, you and your implementation coach will decide on the day of the week and time of day for your regular engagement.

Always remember that this program is designed to work as a partnership, with your success as the only outcome and the only agenda.

Importance of Having an Effective Action Plan

The Million Dollar Support coach will help you develop an effective Inner and Outer Game action plan for raising private money. Because your coach understands the winning strategies and best practices for raising private money, developing this plan will not take days and hours. In just a matter of minutes, you will have enough of a plan to get focused on taking the right actions and moving in the right direction toward your raising-money goals.

Throughout the program, you will continue to update and modify your plans as you take action and receive feedback. This type of fast-cycle, time-planning process allows you to create an effective, actionable plan much quicker, supporting you in making faster progress. It also helps you to operate and take action with more focus on results instead of aimless activity.

You will have weekly contact with your coach, usually through email, to make sure you're making progress toward the actions you agreed to, and to understand or provide some guidance and direction to solutions with any challenges or blocks you need help in resolving. They will work with you to find an agreeable time to discuss the best approach for resolving challenges if the issue is best addressed with a direct conversation.

Using the Power of Group Learning and Team Synergy

Because you are not the only one enrolled in the Million Dollar Coaching Program and striving to implement the winning strategies and best practices for raising more private money, there is a wonderful opportunity to use the power of group learning and team synergy to achieve greater success faster.

Toward that end, the program allows our top performers to apply to participate in small, high-performance teams. The application process is intended to provide a level of screening to identify the top performers, individuals who have shown the commitment necessary to become the best at raising private money. Those accepted into one of the high-performance teams will accelerate their private money results exponentially from the shared learning, the team synergy, and the high level of team support.

The benefits of being a part of a high-performance team should be easy to see because the team is deeply committed to helping you implement the winning strategies and best practices for raising private money, so that you raise more money than you could dream of. Also, another excellent way to use the synergy of the group is for accelerating your learning and enhancing your skills, so you achieve greater results.

Because role-playing is such a great way to become proficient at talking to private money sources, it is highly beneficial to spend a few minutes each day role-playing with a colleague or role-playing partner. In the program, you will be supported in identifying a role-play partner if you are unable to find one. It is a best practice to change role-play partners frequently to keep the process fresh and to ensure that each person gains the maximum benefit from the activity.

The most successful private money raisers are consistently reviewing their current approach and learning new winning strategies and best practices. Make sure that you are in a support program that consistently teaches new private money tools, tips, and techniques. The best programs should provide opportunities to learn and review tools, tips, and techniques for developing your private money-raising skills and enhancing your capabilities. The critical point to look for in any program is a firm and dedicated commitment to continually educate you and to ensure you're staying ahead of the private money game—both the Inner and Outer Games.

If you want to achieve breakthrough raising private money results, hire an Inner Game coach, supported by a team with experts in raising private money to guide you to victory. The following is a model that shows the critical components required to have a successful raising private money program.

Million Dollars Support Program

Million Dollars Support Program

Mentoring Support
Consulting Support
Coaching Support
High-Performance Peer Group (Synergy)
Role-Playing Partner
Support Buddy
Effectiveness Tools, Tips, and Techniques
Membership Resource and Support Site
Raising Private Money Scrips and Workbook

Million Dollar Support Program Exercise One

1. Review the What I want from a Million Dollar Support Program Checklist, marking yes for the type of support you would want. Use the blank rows at the bottom of the document to add any additional items of support you want to be part of your program.
2. Review your yes's and ask yourself what would be the benefit for you and the results you would achieve if you were participating in a private money-raising program that provides that support at a very high level.
3. What action, if any, are you going to take as a result of understanding the benefit of enrolling in a private money-raising support program?

My Million Dollar Support Program Checklist

What I want from a Million Dollar Support Program	Yes
To help me learn how to become a private money magnet.	
To help me create a plan of action for achieving my private money goals.	
To hold me accountable for taking private money actions and achieving results.	
To challenge and push me so that I move beyond my current comfort zone.	
To help me overcome nonproductive habits.	
To provide me support and encouragement.	
To provide me with unbiased and objective feedback.	
To keep me on track, moving forward and making progress toward achieving my private money goal.	
To help me overcome my fears.	
To help me become comfortable with being in front of wealthy people.	

To help me overcome the fear of being rejected.	
To help me in my conversations with rich people (not knowing what to say, sounding stupid, not knowing how to answer a question)	

Answer the following reflective assessment questions after completing the assessment:
1. What insights or aha's did you receive from completing the checklist?
2. What are the most important things that you want from a Million Dollar Support Program?
3. Use the items listed above, along with the items you marked yes to, on your assessment as you search for the right support program for raising private money.
4. Sign up and enroll in a support program, one that satisfies your requirements.

In the next chapter, you will learn the art and science of establishing effective private money communication.

The skills and capabilities to communicate effectively are a major indicator of the amount of private money you will raise. It is a fact that the better you are at communicating with your private money partners and potential money sources, the more money you will raise.

Chapter Six

EFFECTIVE PRIVATE MONEY COMMUNICATION

A KEY TO BEING MORE EFFECTIVE when you are engaged in a conversation with a potential private money source is to allow your *listening* to drive your speaking. This requires that you listen to hear and then understand before you speak.

Your goal is not just to listen to the other person eighty percent of the time and to speak only twenty percent of the time. Your goal and intentions are to truly understand what the other person is trying to communicate to you.

Remember, one of the biggest problems with communication is the illusion that each person understands what the other individual has said, exactly as it is intended. Messages never come across intact but are constantly filtered by the receiver based on their conditioning. Therefore, resist the temptation to assume that you know what the other person is attempting to communicate.

To make sure that you understand what they are saying, you need to ask engaging questions and then follow up with clarifying questions. Here are some examples of clarifying questions:

1. Please tell me more about that.
2. What do you mean by that?
3. Why is that important to you?
4. Can you tell me a little more about that?
5. Let me make sure I have it right.
6. Please explain how that works.
7. What do you see as the impact of that?
8. How do you see that working?

By asking clarifying questions, your speaking will be driven by the information shared in the conversation. It also shows that you are *learning* about them through the ongoing conversation and not driven by any mind chatter as you try to anticipate and create a nifty response. The mind cannot think about two things at the same time, so if you are focused on your next response, you will miss what they are trying to communicate.

To achieve this state of consciousness, you have to release the need to be ahead of the conversation and to drop the need to have a ready-made answer. This will allow you to really engage and connect with the other person and in so doing, you *actually hear* what they are saying.

One tip to help you is to become *fascinated* with what they are saying. Fascination brings on a temporary state of "*super hearing*." You've done this naturally in your past whenever you were involved in a courting ritual. Think back and remember how this new person you were courting could say anything, even something you had no interest in, and it could hold you in rapt attention. In this state of fascination, you naturally asked engaging questions because you were captivated and infatuated.

You don't need to fall in love with your prospects, but realizing that you have the ability to become fascinated by anything if you're properly motivated will help you bring this "super hearing" to your conversations whenever you wish. Being engaged in this way allows you to hear what the other person is saying, and you will hear more than their words. You will read their body language and hear the subtle changes in the tone of their voice. You will also sense their emotions and see their expressions. You'll hear what they say and get what they truly mean because it is so important to the communication process.

Have you ever been in conversation with someone, and at some point, you recited their words back to them to check for understanding? You may have even used the exact words and phrases that they use. However, they looked at you with a puzzled look on their face and quickly told you that what you said was not what they meant.

Communication is much more than a person's words and phrases.

To be more effective in talking with potential private money sources, make sure that you make it a practice of listening to what the whole person is communicating. Make sure that you listen to their words, their tone of voice, and that you also pay close attention to their body language. Allow your updated understanding and awareness to direct your speaking so that your communication connects exactly with what the other person was communicating.

You will be more effective because your communication will be right on topic and in alignment with what they really are sharing and not just what you think they said.

This makes so much sense, but you need to ask yourself what stops you from doing it consistently. A few of the most common reasons are:

1. You're worried about what you will say next.
2. You're worried about what the script tells you to say.
3. You're worried about how you will respond to what they are saying.
4. You're worrying about how to tell them about the deal you have to share.
5. You're worried about looking stupid.

By the way, the word *worry* comes from the German word *wurgen*, which means to have your throat ripped out by a wild dog or wolf. How's that for a visual? This is where the sports term *choking* comes from. Your body chokes off your blood flow, and you don't perform to your natural potential.

Instead of worrying about all that stuff, take a moment and release your negative thinking. Just relax and listen to them as they communicate. Drop your need to figure it out before they say it or ask it. Let the conversation unfold naturally through the course of the discussion. You are not there to be the answer person. You are there to listen, understand, engage, connect, and to truly hear them.

To help you to relax, regardless of your private money-raising experience level, simply say to any question you ever encounter in any such conversation that you don't know the correct answer to, "I'm not sure about that. If it's important to you, I'll be glad to find it out. Is it important to you?"

When you start worrying about yourself and what you will say next, even for just a moment, there is a great chance that you will miss something important in the conversation that they are attempting to communicate.

A slight change in their tone of voice or a shift in their body language gives their words a very different meaning. This mistaken meaning will send you inside of your own head to find a great answer for the wrong question. Don't do that!

Instead, practice the art of listening fully and allow your listening to direct your speaking. When you are unclear about what they are saying, share with them that you do not understand. Ask clarifying questions to make sure that you do understand. It's pointless to guess at what the individual means when it's so simple to just ask them to explain exactly what they do mean. This attention also lets them know that you are truly listening to hear and to understand.

Here is a perfect example that illustrates how your mind chatter can interfere with your listening, and how sometimes you have to put your internal conversation aside to focus on the other person. One of my Private Lender clients shared this powerful teaching story with me.

> This Private Lender just loves to surf. One day, he was out surfing with a handful of other surfers who were having a great time riding the waves to the shore.
>
> As the day wore on, he noticed that all the surfers had left except for him and one other person. So, the two of them paddled out into the ocean, and as they were waiting to catch a wave, they started up a conversation. As they waited for the wave, his fellow surfer asked him what he does for a living.
>
> He answered, "I'm a Private Lender, and I'm very excited about the passive income that I'm making and the free time I have to spend with my family."

Before he could say more, the next wave came in, and he was off surfing it to shore. As he was paddling back out to position himself for the next wave, his mind chatter began and he tried to come up with some clever follow-up response that he could say to the person as they waited for the next wave. His thoughts were:

1. Is this a great time to tell and sell him on my investment opportunity?
2. Should I talk to him about the investment opportunities I have?
3. Should I talk to him about the interest rates that I am able to provide?
4. Should I talk to him about how he can get a bigger return than just interest on my investment opportunity?
5. Should I tell him why being my private money source is so great and wonderful?
6. Should I tell him about the dangers in the stock market and why he should be investing in other opportunities?
7. Is this my first touch or have I seen him before?
8. I think I may have talked with him before.
   His mind chatter continued on and on, and all of a sudden he heard a voice inside of his mind say, "Just relax. Don't feel pressured to turn this into an opportunity to close a deal. Instead, focus on engaging in a conversation and getting to know him. Put raising money aside and connect with him; don't go into telling and selling. Just have a conversation and focus on cultivating the relationship."

While they were waiting for the next wave to come in, the Private Lender decided to work through the relationship-building questions from his conversation starter stack in a relaxed manner in order to connect with the other surfer and understand more about him.

He asked him, "Where do you work?"

The other surfer answered, "I'm a plastic surgeon, and I've been doing it for a number of years. I'm great at it, and I've made a lot of money doing it, but I know it's just a matter of time before my hand won't be steady enough to continue in this line of work. It's been a great career for me, and I love doing it."

The next wave came in, and they surfed to shore. Then they paddled back out to wait for the next wave. The conversation continued. "A plastic surgeon, that's sounds like a great profession! Where do you live?"

The surgeon answered, "Just a few miles from here. I wanted to be close to the ocean, so I can surf more often. My office is not that far from here. Typically, my son is with me. He loves to surf as well, but he couldn't make it today because he has football practice at school."

The next wave came in, and they surfed into shore. As they paddled back out to wait for the next wave, he said to himself, "Just focus on having a conversation and understanding more about this guy and what he's all about." He was building trust through asking questions and being fascinated with the plastic surgeon. He found it very interesting because he really didn't know any plastic surgeons, especially one that had a love of surfing that matched his.

He was following his practice of being interested, listening for the purpose of understanding, and asking relationship-building questions. He had control of his mind chatter, so it was not distracting him from connecting with the plastic surgeon.

As they were waiting on the next wave, he asked, "Do you have any other children?"

The plastic surgeon said that yes, he had a daughter who was also in high school. "She's not big on surfing—she's more of a reader." And he continued, "I've been married for over twenty years, and my wife and I love this area. I'm so glad that I'm able to live close to the ocean and take advantage of all this area has to offer."

Then he asked, "What does your wife do?"

"My wife used to work," the surgeon explained, "but since I've been so successful as a plastic surgeon, she's been able to stay home for a number of years, which gave us the opportunity to provide such a great environment for the kids. She has other interests that keep her excited and involved with the community."

Their discussion continued as they waited for each new wave, and during that time he found out that the plastic surgeon was originally born in Connecticut and moved to California because he felt that a plastic surgeon would do better in California than in Connecticut. His favorite sports team was the 49ers, and he had a golden retriever that he loved.

He continued to ask questions, building rapport and trust by listening, being interested, and engaging in a conversation without telling and selling. He noticed that he no longer felt the internal tension to talk about private lending, private money, or a deal.

A plastic surgeon qualifies as a busy professional, which is exactly the kind of person that he wants to have as a private money partner. He realized that getting to know him, understanding him, and cultivating their relationship was the best course of action to take at this point.

As they were waiting for the next wave, the plastic surgeon said to him, "So, tell me, what is private lending?" A wave came and away they went, and as they were paddling back out, he thought, "My potential private money source has asked me about private lending. Is this my golden opportunity to tell him about, all of the benefits of private lending? Or should I continue to build the relationship and increase my understanding of the plastic surgeon's situation?"

As they were waiting for the next wave he answered the surgeon, "To answer your question, I worked as an executive in Corporate America for over twenty-five years, and I always did well for myself. I enjoyed being an executive manager, and the financial rewards were great.

Just like you, understanding that you can't be a plastic surgeon forever, I got to an age where I wanted to start making sure I could replace my income with other income, so I could maintain my lifestyle as I got closer to retirement.

So, I looked at alternative investments like real estate, and I purchased some income-producing properties. I found out that when compared with three important factors—liquidity, returns, and risk—there is another vehicle that beats income property hands-down in terms of producing income.

I realized quickly that I was either taking too much risk or that I would have to live well below my current standard of living.

Then I found out about private lending. And here's why I love it.

I found it's relatively safer than other investment vehicles when it comes to consistent monthly income.

Today private lending is my main focus, and it is providing me the income I need to maintain my current standard of living.[1]

It is so great surfing with you! I'm having such a great time! When we're done, let's exchange contact information so that we can have coffee or lunch. Then I can explain to you what private lending is and why I'm so excited about it! Perhaps we can coordinate schedules and surf again together. I would love to meet your son."

The plastic surgeon agreed, indicating that he was very interested in hearing all about private lending. They continued to surf until they both were tired.

When they were done surfing and they were walking back to their cars, he asked his new friend, "Do you enjoy reading like your daughter?" The surgeon answered, "I love reading anything about sports." The Private Lender said, "Have you read Bill Walsh's book called *The Score Will Take Care of Itself*? The surgeon said that he had not.

"It's a great book I think you'll like, particularly because you're a 49er fan. The book is all about how Bill Walsh built the 49er's dynasty. It's a very insightful book filled with a lot of useful information on just how he built a Super Bowl dynasty. I have a copy of the book in my trunk that I'd like to give you—I think you'll enjoy it."

---

[1] The script is created by George Antone, taught in The Private Money Code Workshop for more info contact george@fynanc.com

Effective Private Money Communication

The plastic surgeon was very appreciative and thanked him.

The Private Lender gave his copy of the book to the plastic surgeon and included his business card. The plastic surgeon returned the favor, giving him his business card. They agreed to get in contact with each other later in the week to schedule a time to chat about private lending over lunch.

I will let you in on a secret. The Private Lender had many different kinds of books in the trunk of his car. Regardless of the type of book the surgeon liked to read, chances are that the Private Lender would have had a book of that type in his trunk.

If the plastic surgeon had said I love to read murder mysteries, the Private Lender had two of the top murder mystery author's books in his trunk. If the plastic surgeon had said, "I love cooking," the Private Lender had a cookbook or two in his trunk. If the plastic surgeon had said that he enjoyed reading motivational books, you guessed it, the Private Lender had a few of the latest motivational books in his trunk.

The secret is that the Private Lender knows that when you give a person a gift, you activate the science of reciprocity. This means that the other person is looking to give you something in return.

Having books or audio books on CDs to give to potential private money sources is just a side note to the story. The real key is that he was able to resist going into the telling-and-selling mode. Instead, he used the natural rhythm of the ocean to settle him down and get him focused on having a conversation for the purpose of building a relationship and gaining a greater understanding of the potential private money source's needs, wants, and desires.

The next step for him is to make sure that he follows up with the surgeon within the next twenty-four hours to set the appointment. He must not make an excuse to back out of the appointment at the last moment.

The Private Lender took a few minutes to document his contact with the plastic surgeon in his logbook to make sure that he had an accurate record of the date, the time, and relevant facts of the conversation.

The chances are very high that the next time that you run across a busy professional, you will not have the ocean to keep you from going into a telling-and-selling mode. But you can practice releasing the impulse to want to discuss private lending or your deals and instead, focus on establishing a relationship.

This is, after all, the winning strategy and best practice for raising private money.

Listening so that you hear exactly what the other person is saying, letting your updated understanding guide your speaking, and asking clarifying questions to make sure that you get the message correctly are very effective practices for raising private money.

Let Your Listening Drive Your Speaking Exercise:

Take a moment and answer the following Reflective Assessment questions:

1. What can you do to get yourself centered and grounded on conducting a relationship-building conversation when you feel the tension to talk about private lending?
2. What can you do to get yourself to ask more questions when you are talking to potential private money sources?
3. What can you do to become fascinated with your prospect so your questions just naturally flow?
4. What can you do to enhance your listening skills so that you can truly hear and understand what the other person is saying?
5. What can you do to reduce the monkey mind chatter that's going on inside your head when you are trying to listen to someone else?
6. What can you do to stop yourself from trying to anticipate what the person is going to say next?
7. What can you do to keep yourself from turning into the answer person and instead remain interested in what the other person is saying?
8. What insights did you gain, if any, from the exercise?
9. Based on any insights that you gained from the exercise, what actions are you going to take that will increase the amount of private money that you will raise over the next six months?

10. Make a commitment to implement a few of the actions you came up with and then implement them.

In the next chapter, you will learn how to elevate your private money-raising game to a new level that will accelerate the amount of private money you raise by ten times or more.

Chapter Seven

ELEVATE YOUR RAISING PRIVATE MONEY GAME

IT'S TIME TO ELEVATE YOUR private money game to a new level!

I have a powerful and inspiring picture of Michael Jordan slam-dunking a basketball to score the winning points in a very close game.

I have this picture of Michael Jordan hanging on my office wall because clearly he could elevate his basketball game and achieve victory when everything was on the line.

When you think about raising private money, ask yourself, is it time for *you* to elevate *your* game? Please believe me when I say that you really do have the potential to raise more private money than you are currently doing. And it *is* time to elevate your game and raise the private money you need to take your business to the next level.

> **You know many of the winning strategies and best practices for raising private money. Therefore, you have the potential to raise much more private money than you are currently doing.**

The key to elevating your game is to understand exactly what is getting in your way and stopping you from using all of your potential for raising private money.

What Inner Game barriers and challenges are preventing you from elevating your Private Money Game?

When I reflect on my picture of Michael Jordan elevating his game, it serves as a reminder and an inspiration that we all have this unending potential that we could use to achieve our goals.

Potential refers to all of your gained knowledge, experiences, and practiced skills. All that you have learned about raising private money is the essence of your potential.

As you learn more, you increase your potential to use that knowledge for achieving your private money goals. Potential does not mean that you are using what you have to accomplish your goals. It just means that you have the *ability* to achieve more if you used more of your knowledge. If you used more of what you have been taught, your results would increase.

In fact, every time you take a training program, you increase your potential. Every time you learn something from reading a book or an article, it increases your potential in that area.

As you complete the training program on raising private money, you will understand what to do, how to do it, and when to do it. You will have increased your private money raising potential.

The wedge below represents all the potential that you have available to use when raising private money—all of the skills and knowledge you possess.

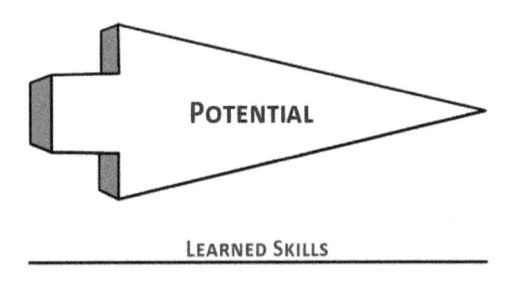

POTENTIAL

LEARNED SKILLS

The image of the wedge below illustrates your actual performance and your current achievement level. It represents how much of your full potential you are actually using to achieve results. It shows just how much of what you know you are actually using.

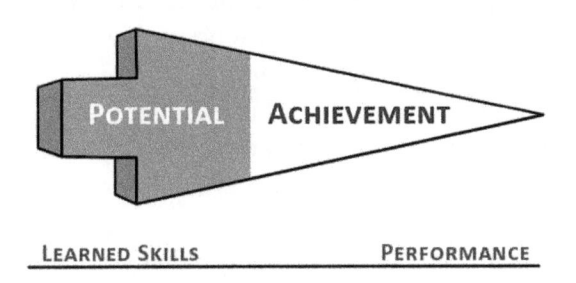

POTENTIAL ACHIEVEMENT

LEARNED SKILLS   PERFORMANCE

It is not how much you know that leads to success. It is how much of what you know that you actually use that determines your level of success.

It follows that it is not how much you know about raising private money that determines the amount of money that you raise. It is how much of what you know that you actually use that determines the amount of money you raise.

Contrary to popular belief, what you achieve is determined, not by your skills or abilities, but by your performance. Your level of achievement is not determined by your potential, but by the actual amount of potential that you use for raising private money.

This image clearly demonstrates that your potential is far greater than your achievement. It also means that you are not raising the amount of private money that you know how to achieve because you are not using your full potential for raising private money.

This gap between your potential and what you are actually using probably exists in every area of your life.

For example, take your health. I guarantee you that you have the knowledge and the skills to live a healthier lifestyle. Therefore, based on your knowledge and skills, you have the potential to live a much healthier lifestyle than you are currently living. However, what you are implementing of what you know is far less than your full knowledge on how to live a healthier lifestyle.

Let's take that example further. It is fairly common knowledge that if you reduce or eliminate salt and sugar from your diet, you will live a healthier lifestyle. It is also common knowledge that increasing the amount of green vegetables that you eat and exercising daily will create a healthier lifestyle.

You have the potential to live a healthier lifestyle than you are currently living, but there is typically a pretty big gap between what you know and what you are implementing.

The point is that your acquired knowledge and skills represents your potential. However, when you examine any area of your life, what you are actually implementing is far less than the potential you possess.

You may find in some areas of your life that you're using as much as 80 percent of your potential. In other areas, you could be as low as

10 percent of your potential. How much of your potential are you actually using for raising private money? To answer that question, complete the raising private money potential utilization self-assessment.

Raising Private Money Potential Utilization Self-Assessment

Please take a few minutes and complete the following raising private money potential utilization self-assessment. Please be honest with yourself as you answer each question:

1. What percent of your raising private money knowledge and skills are you consistently using?
   - Is it 10 percent?
   - Is it 20 percent?
   - Is it 30 percent?
   - Is it 40 percent?
   - Is it 50 percent?
   - Is it 60 percent?
   - Is it 70 percent?
   - Is it 80 percent?
   - Is it 90 percent?
   - Is it 100 percent?

2. List three things below that you know how to do in regard to raising private money that, if you did them consistently, you would raise a lot more private money.

   _____

   _____

3. What support do you need to start implementing the three things you listed above consistently? It is not more knowledge because you already have the knowledge. In other words, you already have the potential to raise much more private money than you are currently doing.

   _____

4. Please complete the Commitment Declaration

Commitment Declaration

On this day _____ *(date)* of _____ *(year)*, I, _____, *(your name)* make a declaration and a commitment to start consistently doing the three things that I've stated above.

The Nine Dot's Exercise:

Take out a blank piece of paper and draw nine dots about an inch apart in the center of the page just like you see here.

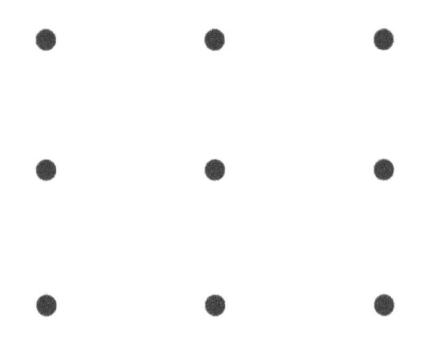

• • •

• • •

• • •

The goal of the exercise is to connect all nine dots with four straight lines, without raising your pen or pencil from the page and without retracing over any line. Once you start to draw, you cannot lift your pen up until you complete your drawing.

Take a few minutes and complete the exercise.

The answer to the exercise is located in the back of the book. Please look up the answer before you continue reading.

See how easy the exercise was? What made the exercise difficult for you was the fact that you did not think you could go outside the box. You believed you had to solve the exercise by drawing inside the box. You thought this even though the instructions didn't say you had to stay inside the box.

Elevate Your Raising Private Money Game

The purpose of this exercise is to demonstrate that what you believe will impact your performance and your results. You had the potential to go outside of the nine dots; you had the potential to think outside of the box, but you didn't because of what you believed about the exercise.

And what you believe about raising private money will impact your ability to use all your knowledge and skills.

Are you implementing all the best practices in regard to raising private money that you have been taught to do? The raising private money actions that you have been taught are so important because they are part of your potential. It is that ability that you can use to raise the amount of private money that you need for your business. Chances are that you're only using about 20–40 percent of what you know about raising private money.

Another reason why I love the mental image of Michael Jordan is because it truly demonstrates the potential that you have to achieve more and to accomplish more. But to do that, you must use more of your private money-raising potential. You must close this gap between potential and achievement. You must close the gap between the skills you have learned and your actual performance. You must elevate your game to take your raising private money to the next level.

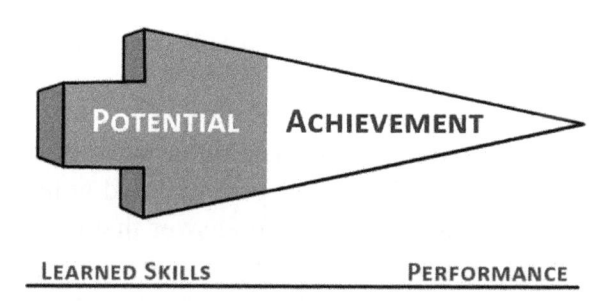

POTENTIAL **ACHIEVEMENT**

LEARNED SKILLS **PERFORMANCE**

I challenge you to look at how much private money you've raised in the last six months and ask yourself: is this reflective of your full potential for raising private money?

Is your actual private money performance reflective of someone that has elevated their raising private money game as though they were in the final seconds of a championship game that they desperately wanted to win?

I know that you are not Michael Jordan, but just as he continued to elevate his basketball game, you too can elevate your raising private money game to achieve championship results.

Are you consistently elevating your private money-raising game?

By now you should understand that you have more potential than you are using; the next obvious question is, what is blocking the use of that potential? All your raising private money training has taught you that you shouldn't be telling and selling when you are having a private money conversation. But do you find yourself doing it anyway?

You know that you should be enrolling potential private money sources by asking engaging questions, but you find yourself talking too much, anyway.

You know that you should be building trust and establishing a foundation to cultivate the relationship, but you find yourself sticking a deal in front of their nose in spite of the fact that you know better. What you often find yourself doing is definitely not what you have been taught to do.

You know that you should be delivering your peak interest statement with excitement and then allowing the other person to talk.

With all this potential, this knowledge of what you should be doing to raise private money, you will still find yourself not doing what you know that you should be doing a very high percentage of the time.

Therefore, the 64,000-dollar question is, what is stopping you from consistently using all of your potential and going full out to become a private money magnet? To answer that question, take a look at the image below. Your identity is one of the major blocks preventing you from using your full potential. Who you see yourself to be will determine how much of your knowledge and your skills you will use for raising private money.

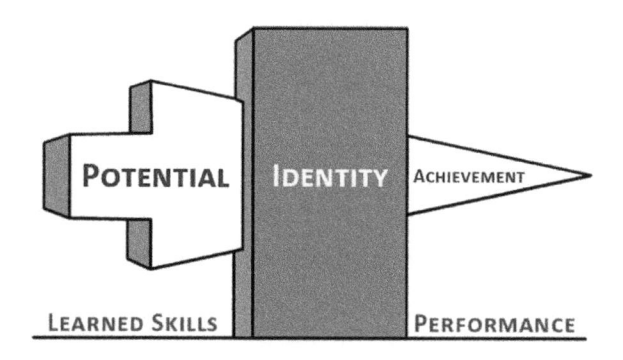

```
POTENTIAL  |  IDENTITY  |  ACHIEVEMENT
LEARNED SKILLS  |         |  PERFORMANCE
```

How you see yourself will determine the approach that you take to raising private money and to conduct your private money conversations. Your approach and the way you conduct private money conversations will determine the level of success you have with your private money sources.

Who you think you are will determine how much of your potential you actually use for raising private money. Your identity can act as a huge block or barrier to your private money success because it will determine how much of your potential you will actually use.

For example, if you see yourself as being successful at raising private money, you will have more success than if you saw yourself as being incapable of raising private money.

If your identity in regard to raising private money is that you are approachable, engaging, and credible, you will have more successful conversations with private money sources. On the other hand, if you see yourself as standoffish, confrontational, and incompetent, more than likely than not, this identity will not serve you well in regard to raising private money.

If you identify yourself as a good networker, there is a high probability that you will do more networking and be more effective at it! If you see yourself as outgoing and friendly, you will definitely follow through on more networking opportunities. Your identity will determine where you go, what you do, the kinds of people who you feel comfortable talking to, the kind of activities that you will engage in, and ultimately, the level of your private money success.

The Inner Game of Raising Private Money

How you identify yourself, who you see yourself to be, will work to block or facilitate the use of more of your potential for raising private money.

The same thing is true about you. Who you believe yourself to be will impact your performance and your approach to raising private money.

What you believe about yourself will impact how you approach raising private money.

What you believe about yourself will impact everything else in your life.

In the next chapter, you will learn what your current private money-raising identity is, how it was formed, and how it is blocking your success.

Chapter Eight

IDENTITY MATRIX: WHO ARE YOU

GIVEN ALL THAT HAS BEEN said, it is very clear that identity plays a very important part in your private money success, as well as success in every area of your life.

It is then important to understand, where does identity come from, and how did you get your identity?

Toward that end, I highly recommend a great book by Marshall Goldsmith that discusses the importance of identity. The title of the book is, *MOJO: How to Get it, How to Keep it, How to Get It Back if You Lose it*. In the book, the author talks about the impact your identity has on your performance and the results that you achieve.

So I ask you again. Who are you? Who do you think you are?

The question of who you are is a very complex one. There is no one, right answer to the question of who you are, but the question does cause you to stop and think. You need to really think about it before you answer.

Goldsmith developed an identity matrix shown below to help you answer the question: Who are you? I love 2 by 2 matrixes because they can really help you understand and then answer very complex questions. His identity matrix helps you to not only understand your identity, but how your identity can block you or support you in using more of your private money-raising potential.

```
            FUTURE
              ◆
    OTHER ◆◆◆◆ SELF
              ◆
            PAST
```

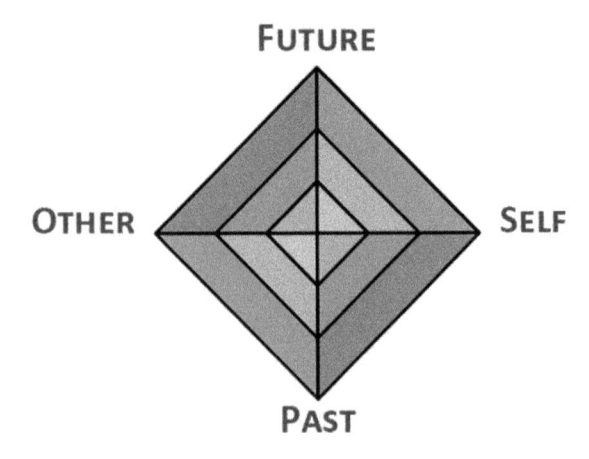

In his book, Goldsmith explains that your identity consists of four dimensions. Your past and your future represent two of the dimensions in his matrix. Your past identity is determined by what you believe you have done in the past. Also to some extent your vision of a future self impacts your identity as well. Both your past identity and your future identity will impact your current performance and your results.

Take out a piece of paper and create your own matrix. On the vertical axis of the matrix, at the top, write the word *Future* and at the bottom write the word *Past*.

He goes on to explain that what you think and believe about yourself and what others think and believe about you impacts your identity. To complete the matrix, on the horizontal axis of the matrix, write the word *Other* on the left side and on the right side of the horizontal axis of the matrix write the word *Self*. The words Self and Other represent the remaining two dimensions in the identity matrix.

Check to make sure that your 2 x 2 matrix matches the image above.

By following this process, you will create an identity matrix that consist of four quadrants. Each of the four quadrants has its own label. Starting at the lower right quadrant, add the words *Remembered Identity*, and on the lower left quadrant add *Reflected Identity*. On the upper left quadrant, add the words *Programmed Identity* and in the upper right quadrant, add the words *Created Identity*.

THE IDENTITY MATRIX

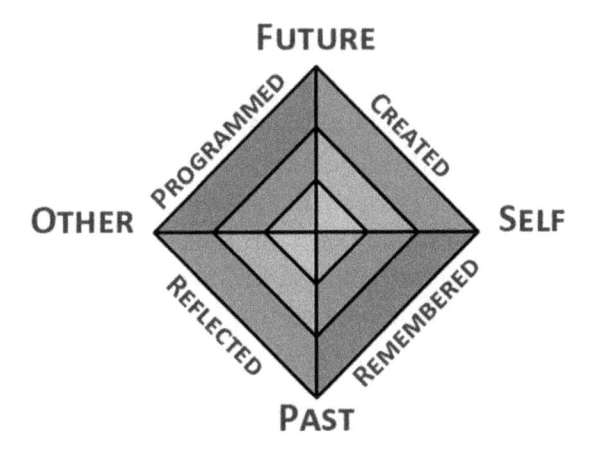

FUTURE

PROGRAMMED · CREATED

OTHER — **SELF**

REFLECTED · REMEMBERED

PAST

Let's examine each of these identities in the matrix to make sure that you have a good understanding of them and how they are formed.

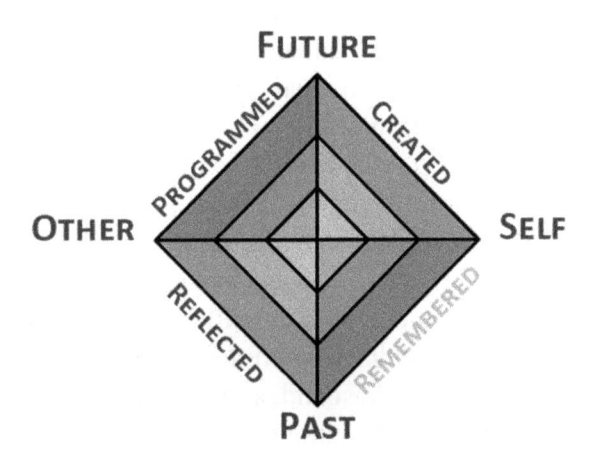

FUTURE

PROGRAMMED · CREATED

OTHER — **SELF**

REFLECTED · REMEMBERED

PAST

Starting with the lower right quadrant, your Remembered Identity are things that you remember from your past about yourself, things that you believe about yourself that you've created from the situations, events, and things that have happened to you in the past.

This past Remembered Identity consists of the things that you keep replaying in your mind, and the things that you believe to be true about yourself, both positive and negative, as a result of past experiences.

In addition, you believe that these past events—real or imaginary—reflect who you are, and to some extent, who you will be as you move forward into the future. One way to look at this is to view your entire life as a book, and each chapter represents one of the many identities that you have had throughout your lifetime. For example, I was born in a small farming community in Southern California. I grew up working on a farm, working in the fields. So, at that time, my identity was that of a farm worker. Since I worked in the fields doing manual labor, I concluded that I wasn't very smart. This was my perception and my self-imposed identity that I reminded myself of each and every day, either consciously or subconsciously.

When I dropped out of high school and went into the military, I was a soldier. At that time, one of my identities was that of a high school dropout. The other was that of a Sergeant in the Army.

When I left the military, my identity became that of a civilian. Since I had not attended a college or university, my identity was not of someone that was well educated. I started working for Chrysler on the assembly line, doing manual labor and making automobiles, part of my identity at the time.

When I got my degree in computer technology and my MBA from the University of Pittsburgh, I was considered educated, and in some circles, I was perceived as being smart.

I find it useful to think of life as chapters in a book, with each chapter representing an identity or identities that you had taken on during that time. Yes, you have multiple identities at any particular time. For example, I was a husband, a father, and a vice president in a major corporation all at the same time.

Each of these activities or events was a very important part of my identity at the time, and they were all based on things I remembered about myself. These opinions that I held of myself formed an identity which impacted my behaviors, my actions, and my results.

Your Remembered Identity consists of the things that you remember about your past that you accept as being who you are and that have become a part of your identity. This Remembered Identity will shape your behaviors, your actions, what you do, what you don't do, impacting your results.

Here's the tricky thing about your Remembered Identity: whether you remember positive things or negative things about yourself, as long as you take them to be who you are, they become a limit on the use of your potential because your potential is much greater than what you have done in the past.

Your past does not determine your future. Your past does not determine the level of private money that you are able to raise unless you accept it as who you are and who you will be.

Remembered Identity Exercise

1. Take a few minutes and select a Remembered Identity from your past that is negatively impacting your ability to raise more private money today. It must be an activity, event, or a situation from your past that is still part of your current identity. (For example, say that you remember that you were not good at networking in the past. Therefore, today, when you think of yourself, you do not see yourself as a networker or being any good at it. As a result of that Remembered Identity, you do not network as much as you should to build the private money sources you require.)
2. What is your Remembered Identity?
3. How does that Remembered Identity negatively impact your performance at raising private money?
4. How does that poor performance negatively impact the amount of private money that you raise?
5. Given what you now know about your Remembered Identity, what will you do differently?
6. List one new action that you will take in the future to support you in raising more private money?
7. Schedule that new action into your calendar or organizer and complete the new action when the time comes.

If you saw yourself differently, for example, as an expert networker or someone that really enjoyed networking, then your attitude in regard to networking would be different, your networking actions would be different, and your private money results would also be very different.

Let's continue our identity matrix discussion by moving to the lower left quadrant that refers to your Reflected Identity, the quadrant that addresses your past and others.

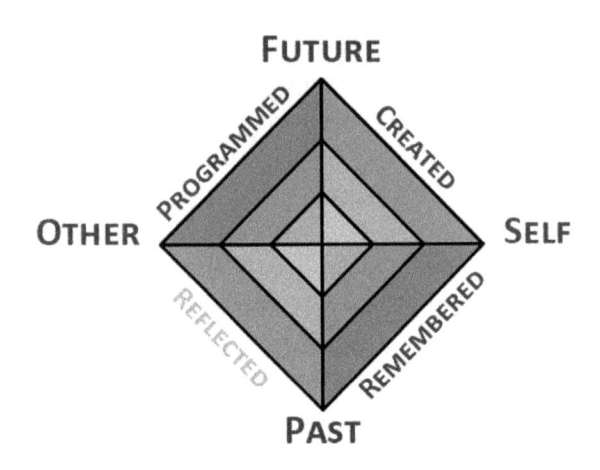

```
                          FUTURE
                    PROGRAMMED  CREATED
         OTHER                           SELF
                    REFLECTED  REMEMBERED
                           PAST
```

Your Reflected Identity consists of the things from your past that the people around you keep reminding you of. They are the things that people keep asking you, "Do you remember when you did this or when you did that?" Quite often, the things that people are pointing out are the negative things you did, the activities, events, or situations that happened in your life. They may sometimes point out positive things that you did or happened to you, but it seems that they have much more fun reflecting on the negative events that happened in your life.

Whenever people around you keep reminding you of past events and you accept those statements as being a part of who you are, they create your Reflected Identity. The people around you keep reflecting this identity back to you because that is who they see you to be. Perhaps that is who they feel you will always be. To them your past determines your future. But for this to become part of your identity, you must agree with the assessment that they keep reflecting back to you, you must accept it as being who you are and who you will be. Your buy-in is required for this to become a part of your Reflected Identity.

For example, whenever I'm around my brothers, they always remind me that I'm the baby in the family. This is so funny because I'm over fifty years old. It's easy for me to discount that reflected identity.

On the other hand, when I'm around people who knew me when I was a vice president at a major corporation, they are disappointed when I tell them what I'm doing now. In their eyes, I've taken a step backward from being someone in a high-powered position to someone with much less power, influence, and control.

It doesn't matter to them that I feel great about what I'm doing. They still see me as the corporate executive with the power over many people's lives with a revenue budget in the millions.

If I let their opinion of me impact how I see myself, it would be hard for me to feel good about what I am doing because I don't manage an organization with thousands of people reporting to me, and I'm not responsible for achieving a revenue budget of over 500 million dollars. That was all a different time and a different chapter in my life.

The positive or the negative things from your past do not have to impact or limit what you achieve in the future.

The future is a creation.

The past does not determine your future. You have the potential to be bigger than anything that you have done before.

You have the ability to reject the Reflected Identity and opinions of others. Even though they may be reminding you of less than desirable memories of the past, you do not have to take that on as being who you are or who you will be. Instead, you can view it as something that you did in the past, but it is no longer a reflection of who you are today or who you will become.

Always remember that, regardless of whether the things from your past are positive or negative, they do not have to impact or limit the results you achieve in the future.

Whether they are things you're saying to yourself that you remember, or things that other people keep reminding you of, they do not have to determine your performance or your results in regard to raising private money or achieving any goal that you set. What you achieve and what you accomplish today is determined by you now, not by your past.

Neither Remembered Identity nor Reflected Identity have to determine your future.

The future is truly a creation.

Both Remembered and Reflected Identities are a function of the past that you have to release and let go of, to use more of your private money-raising potential. If not, it will continue to block you from raising more private money than you are currently doing. To become the private money magnet that you are destined to be, you must release both Remembered and Reflected Identities.

The fact that you have not been good at networking in the past has nothing to do with your potential to be an effective networker today. Just because the people around you tell you that you have never been good at networking does not mean that you will not be effective at networking. Other's reflected identities of you will not have a negative impact on your performance unless you allow their negative beliefs to influence your current networking behaviors.

Your behaviors and actions will always be consistent with your identity and with the person that you see yourself to be.

The upper-left quadrant is entitled Programmed Identity, referring to the messages that you picked up in regard to who you are from your parents and authority figures when you were growing up, including what was being communicated from the environment in regard to you and people like you.

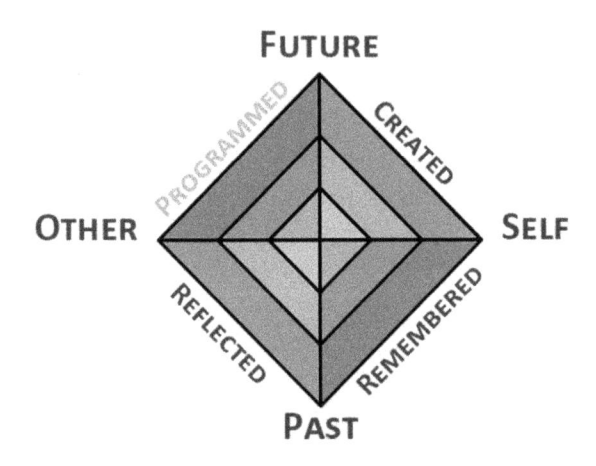

Identity Matrix: Who Are You

All of these messages provided a certain level of programming that contributes to your understanding of who you are and, thus, became part of your Programmed Identity.

There is a strong belief that your identity today was programmed into you between the ages of seven and twelve because that was the time that you were value programmed. That value programming was based on where you were physically located in the world and the unique messages that were being communicated in that environment at that time.

This value programming consisted of what was being said about you and the people who you identified with. This value programming will determine how you see yourself, who you think you are, and how you will act and behave as an adult.

For example, between the ages of seven and twelve, I worked in the fields, so my value programming was that of a farm worker. That was firmly affixed in my identity; it was who I saw myself to be and how I projected myself to be in the future.

That Programmed Identity would definitely have impacted my potential if I had bought into the notion that all I would ever be is a farm worker. I would not have thought of pursuing any other profession that did not involve agriculture if I had believed that my destiny was to become a farm worker.

Armed with an identity of a farm worker, I would not think of becoming a doctor, a lawyer, an astronaut, or a vice president if I did not override the environmental programming that was strongly entrenched in my mind.

Reflected Identity Exercise

1. Take a few minutes and select a negative activity, event, or situation from your past that the people around you keep reminding you of. It could be something that you did or did not do. It must be something that is negatively impacting your ability to raise private money today. It must be an activity, event, or situation from your past that is still part of your current identity. (For example, people around you keep reminding you of the time that you lost someone's money or

a time that you had major investment losses yourself. Part of your identity is the fear that you will lose someone's money if they invested their private money in one of your deals. As a result of that Reflected Identity, you procrastinate on engaging your warm market or busy professionals in private money conversations because you "know" they will not trust you.)
2. What is the Reflected Identity that people keep reminding you of?
3. How does that Reflected Identity negatively impact your private money-raising performance?
4. How does that performance negatively impact the amount of private money that you raise?

Take a few minutes and ask yourself the following Reflective Assessment Questions:
1. What opinions are you accepting from others that are limiting your view of who you are and what is possible for you to achieve in regard to raising private money?
2. What are the negative things that people around you are saying that reinforces your doubts about your abilities to raise private money?
3. What reoccurring negative messages, themes, or comments that you've heard are negatively impacting your self-confidence in regard to raising private money?
4. What are some of the positive reoccurring messages that you keep hearing in regard to your ability to raise private money?
5. What insights did you gain from the exercise and answering the Reflective Assessment Questions?
6. What actions are you going to take to raise more private money?
7. When are you going to complete those actions?

Programmed Identity Reflective Assessment Questions

1. What were the messages that were being programmed into you when you were growing up?

Identity Matrix: Who Are You

2. What were the messages that you heard consistently about you and people like you when you were growing up?
3. What messages did you pick up in regard to who you were from your parents and close relatives when you were growing up?
4. What messages did you pick up from school, from church, and from other organizations you might have participated in regard to who you were?
5. What messages did you pick up about who you were from industries that you worked in?
6. What messages did you pick up concerning who you were from TV programs, movies, and other forms of media?
7. What are two core messages that you picked up from your parents, organizations, industries, TV programs, and other forms of media that are negatively impacting your ability to raise private money?

_____

_____

8. What insights did you gain, if any, from the exercise?
9. Based on any insights that you gained from the exercise, what actions are you going to take that will increase the amount of private money that you will raise over the next six months?

Your Remembered Identity, your Reflected Identity, and your Programmed Identity can be carried forward into the future as who you see yourself to be—if you let it. The choice is totally up to you.

Your potential to raise more private money is greater than any past identity that you have locked onto as being you.

Before you can release your old, outdated identity, you must understand what that identity is and how it was created, and then you'll be able to use more of your Raising Private Money Potential.

In the next chapter, you will learn how to create a new winning identity, one that supports you in raising all the private money you need, want, and desire.

Chapter Nine

CREATING A WINNING PRIVATE MONEY IDENTITY

THE UPPER-RIGHT QUADRANT IS REFERRED to as your Created Identity, which says that you have the ability to create an identity that is consistent with what you choose to be. You are not limited to your Remembered, Reflected, or even your Programmed Identity. You can create the identity that you desire, one that will serve you in becoming the person that you choose to be.

You have the power to create who you are.

You have the power to overrule what you have done in the past.

You have the power to ignore and discount what others are saying and have said about who you are.

You have the ability to invent the identity that you choose, one that will serve you in becoming the person that you desire to be.

You can create an identity that will allow you to be successful at raising more private money with ease.

This Created Identity will allow you to use more of your full potential to achieve any goal you desire.

Your ability to create your identity gives you the flexibility to continually change, modify, and adjust your identity to match the new private money goals that you seek.

Your Created Identity allows you to unlock the full use of your potential so that you can achieve extraordinary results.

As you expand your identity, it will free up your potential, and you will find yourself doing the things that are necessary to significantly increase the amount of private money that you raise.

The truth is, you act and behave like the person you see yourself to be. Therefore, if you change your identity to one of a person that is very successful at raising private money, you will start taking more of the appropriate actions to increase the amount of private money you raise.

Your ability to create your own identity is the key to having more private money success.

At one point in my life, I created a new identity for myself, one of a person who could be an effective vice president. And that Created Identity supported me in using much more of my full potential to achieve my career goal. The same thing is true for you when it comes to raising more private money. In fact, when you create an identity consistent with raising more private money, you will unlock your potential and raise more private money than you are currently achieving.

Here are just a few things that must be part of your private money-raising identity if you are to unlock and use more of your potential:
- You must see yourself as someone capable of building trust when you are talking to your potential private money sources.
- You must see yourself as someone capable of adding value and benefit to your potential private money sources.
- You must see yourself as someone capable of delivering a peak interest statement that generates excitement in your private money sources.
- You must see yourself as having influence with your potential private money sources.
- You must see yourself as someone who can develop and cultivate long-term relationships with potential private money sources.

Your past does not have to determine your future. You choose to create your future by the actions that you consistently take.

Created Identity Exercise

1. Take a moment and complete the following exercise.
2. What identity would best support you in raising more private money?
3. What identity will unlock more of your raising private money potential?
4. What identity will turn you into a private money magnet?
5. What identity do you need to be successful at raising much more private money than you are currently doing?
6. What are the things from your Remembered Identity that are impacting your raising private money ability?
7. What are the things from your Reflected Identity that are impacting your ability to raise private money?
8. What are the things from your Programmed Identity that are impacting your ability to raise more private money?

If these negative thoughts are consistently playing inside your mind, they will block the use of your private money-raising potential. Understanding the messages playing inside of your mind allows you to overcome them because you realize that they're from the past, and the past does not determine your future unless you let it.

External Created Identity Exercise

It is important to make sure that everything that refers to you or describes who you are is consistent with your Created Identity, the identity that will support you in raising more private money. One of your first actions after completing this chapter is to make sure that all your social media sites and profiles reflect your Created Identity. This includes:
- Your website
- Your Facebook profile
- Your LinkedIn profile
- All search-engine information found via Google and other search engines

Creating a Winning Private Money Identity

- Other social media, electronic media, and print media information.
- In fact, all of the external information describing who you are and what you do must be changed to reflect your new and effective raising private money identity.

Your goal is to keep checking and updating all of your social media sites and any other forms of documentation to ensure that they are consistent with your Created Identity.

Now that you have completed the Identity Matrix, you understand that the past does not have to determine your future, that the future is a creation, and that your identity will impact your ability to use more of your potential.

A key question becomes, "How can you release the past to create your new identity so you can achieve your raising private money goal?"

I know many of you are saying, "I hope that he doesn't bring up affirmations and how affirmations can help you change and rewrite your new identity." Before answering, let me give you a short test.

> **Finished files are the result of years of scientific study combined with the experience of many years of experts.**

Take a few seconds to read through the sentence above. Now, go back and read through it again. This time, I want you to count the number of letter F's in the sentence.

How many F's did you see? How many F's did you count?

Once you have counted the number of F's in the statement and you have your answer, then and only then read the correct answer recorded on the answer sheet at the end of the book.

If you are like most people you did not see all the F's.

Why is it you could not see all of the F's? Probably because of your past conditioning. Typically, the better reader you are, the more likely you were to see three or four F's because your conditioning is so strong that you read "ov" when seeing the word *of* (pronouncing the word as if it had a V). When your mind looks at the word, it reads right over it and automatically puts the "o-v" there.

Here is a great question: where is the "o-f" stored, the "o-v"? Where does that translation from o-f to o-v happen? Understanding that is the key to changing, releasing, and updating your stored memory so that you can change your identity and become more effective. If you knew where that "of" and "ov" was stored, you could release the old, outdated identity. You can add to your identity, or you can change your identity to one that supports you in achieving your goals.

Where is your identity stored? Where in the brain?

To answer that question, I am going to take you through the *process of thought*. Realize that the brain is one integrated whole, but I am going to describe the brain in three sections and discuss the purpose of each component separately.

Conscious Mind

- Perception
- Association
- Evaluation
- Decision

First, you perceive something as it comes through your conscious mind, the first component. Your conscious mind helps you to perceive, to associate, evaluate, and make decisions.

When you see something, you *perceive* what it is, and you *associate* by asking yourself, "Have I seen anything like this before?" You *evaluate* what it is, where it's probably leading you, and then you make a *decision*.

The information and what you perceive and associate is connected with your subconscious mind, the second component. Think of your subconscious mind as a huge recording machine, a storage device that stores everything that is happening to you, everything that you think has happened to you, and every thought and feeling that you have ever had. It's all recorded and stored within your subconscious mind.

Subconscious Mind

- Recording mechanism
- Stores your interpretation of reality

Every moment from the time you were born and every minute along the way, your subconscious mind continually records everything. That is why a brain surgeon can cause you to remember things from your childhood by touching a certain spot in your brain. You can remember things that you heard and things that you had forgotten. You can remember things that you had done when you were five years old! It's all stored there in your subconscious mind.

The storage area of the subconscious mind is divided into two parts. One part declares, "This is who you are and what your reality is." The other part, "This is not like you; it is not the person you see yourself to be but is part of your potential."

The third component is your creative, subconscious mind. This is the command center. This is where your self-image and your identity are stored. The creative subconscious controls your behavior, it releases creativity to solve problems, and it also provides you with the drive and the energy to move toward your goal.

Creative Subconscious Mind

- Command center
- Maintains your self-image
- Controls behavior
- Creatively solve problems
- Provides you with the drive and energy necessary to achieve a goal

When you see the word "of" while reading, you perceive it through the conscious mind. The "of" then gets recorded in your subconscious mind, and that information is shared with your creative subconscious mind as well.

The creative subconscious is the command center whose job it is to keep you operating consistently with who you see yourself to be.

In the command center, the "o-f" would be stored as "o-v." Therefore, when you perceive "o-f" through your conscious mind, it is also recorded in your subconscious mind.

The conscious mind asks the creative subconscious mind what it sees in the sentence. The creative subconscious mind, acting as the command center, will compare your reality with your potential, and in this case communicates that it sees "ov," and not "of."

It does this because you have been conditioned to read "of" as "ov." That conditioning creates your reality, and that reality affects the words you see on a page. Your conditioning also determines the events you see in your life and even the private money opportunities you see and which ones you act on.

The creative subconscious mind will see the "o-f" and say, "It's not an f, it's an ov," and will communicate to the subconscious mind that it is not a f. And all of a sudden, what you see through your conscious mind is not an f. Therefore, you only see two or three f's. You don't see the standalone of's; you miss them. This is how the command center works to maintain your sanity.

Where is your identity stored? Your identity, who you see yourself to be, is stored in your creative subconscious mind.

Let us say that your identity is that you are not good at networking. Then you see a networking opportunity. You perceive that opportunity through your conscious mind. You store the networking opportunity in your subconscious mind. The subconscious mind communicates the networking opportunity to your creative subconscious mind, the command center. Then the creative subconscious mind communicates back to the subconscious mind that you're not good at networking. That is not like you, and therefore, networking is not recorded as part of your core identity.

With that command from the creative subconscious, your conscious mind would evaluate that information and ask, "What is this networking opportunity leading me toward?" and you would make a decision. That decision would most likely be, "I don't think I'll go networking to meet new private money sources."

The creative subconscious mind is the command center because it actually controls what you see. It also controls what you do so that you keep acting consistent with yourself, consistent with the image or the picture that is stored in your subconscious mind of who you see yourself to be.

It is very important to understand that the primary role of your creative subconscious mind is to keep you taking actions that are consistent with how you identify yourself. It also provides the drive, energy, and motivation necessary to take actions that are "like you."

If you changed how you identify yourself, your creative subconscious mind would provide the drive, the energy, and the motivation to make sure that you acted and behaved consistently with the new picture.

This is the positive benefit to having the mind work the way it does, because by changing the picture in your subconscious mind to match the picture of the person you want to be, the person that you need to be to achieve your private money goal will emerge naturally.

Guess what? Once you change your identity, your picture of who you see yourself to be, you would automatically act like that new person without any effort.

Think of that.

That is so powerful.

Your creative subconscious mind will move you toward the new picture without any conscious effort on your part. That is why the creative subconscious mind is so important for you to raise more private money and for you to become a private money magnet.

The creative subconscious is such an integral part of determining how you operate, where you go, what you do, and how effective you are at any activity you perform, and certainly, how effective you will be when it comes to raising private money.

Now you know where your identity, who you think you are, is stored. You can change that identity. How do you get the picture in your subconscious mind that you want? If you think back to the identity matrix, these pictures, these identities, were collected and put in there through various ways. They were put in through your Remembered Identity, your Reflected Identity, your Programmed Identity, and even to some degree through your Created Identity.

In order to move to the next level of raising private money, you need to put an updated identity in your subconscious mind, one that is consistent with whom you need to be so that you can achieve your private money goals.

Some people will say that affirmations are absolutely the key to changing the picture, the identity in your subconscious mind to the one that you want. I agree that affirmations, visualizations, and experiencing the new you are important. But most people do not handle affirmations, visualization, and experiencing correctly because they don't take into consideration the evolution of the brain.

I know that many of you reading this book did not think that we would spend so much time on the process of thought and the brain. However, understanding how the brain works is the key to changing your private money-raising identity to make it match your desired goals.

EVOLUTIONARY HISTORY OF THE BRAIN

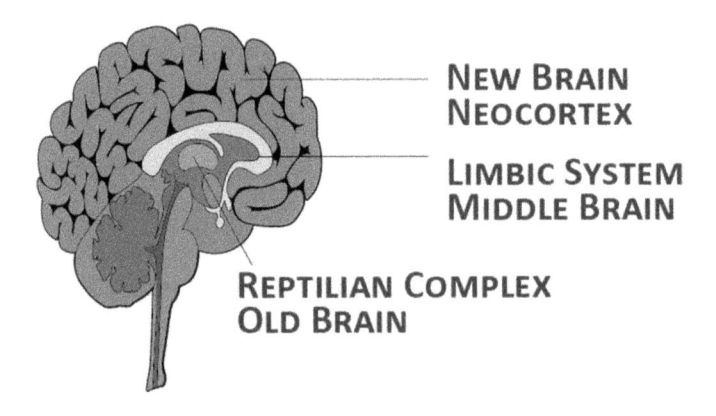

NEW BRAIN
NEOCORTEX

LIMBIC SYSTEM
MIDDLE BRAIN

REPTILIAN COMPLEX
OLD BRAIN

Let us think of the brain as having three phases of evolution. Each evolutionary phase became its own brain. The first evolutionary phase is the reptilian brain, which is preoccupied with your survival. When you remember the image of Maslow's Hierarchy of Needs, the lowest level of need is that of survival. Think of this brain as focused on how-do-I-survive, and how-do-I-avoid-pain. Many people call this the caveman brain because the caveman was focused on how-do-I-avoid-getting-eaten? That was his highest, and some think it was the only, priority. The caveman was not focused on being happy and having fun. Life for the caveman was all about survival. In fact, all the positive thinking and fun-loving cavemen died off early. So the cavemen learned to be preoccupied with danger, to be preoccupied with the things that could kill them.

The reptilian is a very negative processing brain. Have you ever wondered why you have more negative thoughts than positive thoughts each day? The reptilian brain is at the heart of those negative thoughts because it has to continually look out for danger and be suspicious of everything in order to survive. If you were a positive thinking, optimistic caveman, you may have tried to pet or ride a dinosaur. It's a good thing that the caveman brain was so negative or mankind would have died off. The reptilian brain is still inside of you and is still carrying the legacy of focusing on survival, negative thoughts, and a strong need to avoid pain.

The next brain, the middle brain, is the limbic system. It focuses on rewards. You can think of this part of the brain reacting as a mouse would when it is put into a maze. If you placed a piece of cheese somewhere in the maze, the mouse will run the maze to find the cheese. That is what motivates this particular part of the brain. The limbic system is looking for rewards and gains. It's not worried about survival, and it's not trying to avoid pain. Instead, it's seeking rewards and gains.

Finally, the neocortex is the outer brain (the new brain). The neocortex is really focused on authenticity, connecting with others, making a contribution to others, and relationships. This part of the brain is preoccupied with the "why" behind the actions or goals.

When you want to change that picture that is stored in your subconscious mind to match the identity that you need to achieve your goal, you have to change all three brains and not just one. Therefore, your affirmations, visualizations, and experiences must address the needs and requirements of all three brains to impact your reality, who you see yourself to be.

When you identify a behavior that you are doing that does not match the action necessary to achieve your private money goal, you must describe the negative consequences for not taking that action before your reptilian brain will support the correct action. For example, if you are not networking to build trusting relationships with potential private money sources, you must provide pain for your reptilian brain to support you. Otherwise, it will be working against your desires because its primary concerns are with surviving and avoiding pain.

Remember the reptilian part of your brain is going to be driven to move away from the pain.

If you are serious about taking new actions and raising more private money, you must make the consequences of staying the same appear painful to the reptilian brain. By identifying the negative consequence for staying the same or not taking the new actions required to achieve your goal, that pain will motivate you to take the right actions, such as networking to meet new private money sources.

You have to make the consequences real to the reptilian brain; otherwise, you are wasting your time. What are the negative consequences for not networking consistently to meet new private money sources? The following are a few examples of the negative consequences for not networking:

1. You do not have a financially successful private lending business.
2. You do not have the income that you need to live the lifestyle that you desire.
3. You are not able to pay all your bills and save money for your kid's education.
4. You are not able to pay your mortgage, and therefore, you lose your home.
5. Your kids are not able to attend college or the college that they want.
6. You don't have the money you need to pay for the proper amount of medical coverage for your family.
7. You don't have the financial resources you need to live the lifestyle that you desire.
8. You have to work all the time to make enough money to live on, which is prohibiting you from spending quality time with your family.
9. Your colleagues have lost their confidence in you because you are not able to achieve your private money-raising obligations to the company.

10. Every time you look in the mirror, you see a person who is failing at raising private money, and this reality is killing you.

By now it should be very clear that you need the negative consequences of losing your home before the reptilian brain will support you in networking. Your reptilian brain will say, "I don't want to lose my home. That would be so painful. I don't want to experience that loss or pain, so I am going to move away from it. I am definitely going to that networking event tonight."

This is just one part of the new picture that you must place in your subconscious mind to get started networking for more private money sources.

To keep you moving forward and networking, you must also address the needs of the limbic system, which is focused on personal gain. It's highly motivated by achieving rewards, so therefore, part of your affirmation, visualization, and experiencing process must identify the specific reward that you will receive by the raising the private money goal or result.

The limbic system reacts like a mouse will when it is put in a maze with some cheese. Therefore, it asks you to state in your affirmation, "What will you get if you complete the maze? What is the specific reward you will receive when you find the maze's exit? What is the specific reward you will receive as a result of your consistent networking?"

The following are some examples of affirmations that satisfy the needs of the limbic system:
1. I have established five new private money sources.
2. I have raised $200,000 in private money from the people I met through networking.
3. I have invested that $200,000 of private money and received $30,000 as a result.
4. I used part of that $30,000 to pay off my debt and to take my mate on a Hawaiian vacation.
5. I have a private lending business that is growing by 50 percent year over year. As a result of consistent growth, my business is financially strong.

6. My $20,000 a month cash flow supports me in living my desired lifestyle.

By adding these type of statements to your affirmations, visualizations, and experiencing processes, your limbic system will have the motivation to provide the drive and energy for you to engage in more networking events for the purpose of connecting with new private money sources.

The next part of your affirmation, visualization, and experiences must address the needs of the neocortex, which is motivated by a deep need to understand the following:
1. Why do you want to achieve your goals for raising private money?
2. Why is it important to achieve your goals for raising private money?
3. What will be different in your life as a result of achieving your goals for raising private money?
4. How will you feel when you achieve your goals for raising private money?
5. How will achieving your private money-raising goals contribute to the lives of others?
6. How will achieving your private money goals build a stronger connection with the people you care about?
7. How will achieving your private money goals benefit the lives of others?
8. How will achieving your private money goals enhance the quality of your relationships?

Remember that the neocortex needs a much bigger cause, a bigger reason why, than just pain or gain.

The Neocortex is motivated by a deep need to understand "the Why" behind the goal.

Your affirmation, visualization, and experiencing process must have a very sensory-rich "why" to activate the neocortex so that it provides the drive and motivation to take new actions, such as networking and reaching out to busy professionals.

The key to changing your identity is to update your command center by using affirmations, visualizing, and experiences. But your affirmations need to be constructed to address the needs and concerns of all three brains: the reptilian brain, the limbic system, and the neocortex.

Your visualizations require that you vividly imagine and experience the concerns that the reptilian brain requires and wants to move away from (feel the pain), the reward that the limbic system needs (rewards and gains) and therefore wants to move toward, and a very strong, emotional, and big "why" that the neocortex wants to experience before your brain turns on the strong drive and energy required to move forward with new actions.

When your affirmation statement embodies all three brains' needs and you visualize, imprint, and experience the private money-raising identity as though it has been achieved, you will start taking more aggressive actions that move you toward your new private money goal.

Affirmations are the key to changing your identity to the one that you want.

Remember, you will only affirm and visualize the pain part of your statement once or twice a day. You will visualize the other parts of your affirmation statements, the reward and the why statement, six times a day for sixty days. That way, you will move toward that goal faster because you have rewritten the outdated and limiting information in your command center.

This process of internal change is effective and powerful because each of your imprinting visualizations will rewrite over your old identity of, "I'm not good at networking. I'm not a networker. I'm not good at building trust." Instead it will rewrite in your command center, "I'm good at networking, I'm good at building trust, and I'm good at raising private money." That process is the key to changing that picture, your identity, and releasing that old, outdated identity of who you are.

To change your identity, you must write new information into your creative subconscious. It's always managing your behaviors to ensure they're consistent with who you see yourself to be. You need t new picture of yourself to take new actions that move you forward toward your goal or results.

Read, visualize, imprint, and vividly imagine the new affirmation four times a day. Take the time to create the affirmation statements that will allow you to move toward creating that identity.

The following process will support you in releasing your outdated picture of yourself and embrace an effective private money raiser's identity, one that is in alignment with raising all the private money you want, need, and desire.

Please take the time to complete the following questions and create your new raising private money identity.

1. What amount of private money do you want to raise during the next eighteen months? What is your private money-raising goal?
2. Why do you want to raise this amount of private money?
3. Why is it important to achieve your private money goal?
4. How will achieving your private money goal positively impact your life?
5. How will you feel when you have achieved your private money goal?
6. What are the negative consequences if you don't achieve your private money goal?
7. How will you feel if you do nothing differently in regard to raising private money than you are currently doing and as a result your life remains exactly the same?
8. Given that you are committed to achieving your private money goal, what action will you take to do so?
9. Schedule time in your calendar to take the actions listed above.

Creating a Winning Identity Exercise

The following process will support you in creating a new winning raising private money identity, one that is aligned with your private money financial goals. Also, the process will help you change any limiting beliefs that you hold in regard to raising private money.

The process is effective because it addresses the needs of all three brains, which makes lasting change a reality for you.

Let's get started with creating your new winning, private money-raising identity.

It is best to write your responses to each question on a separate sheet of paper because your answers will become statements that you must read, visualize, and experience each day, in order to achieve lasting change in your behaviors, in your performance, and in your results.

Before you complete the exercise, review the creating a winning identity example below.

Creating a Winning Identity Example

1. *What aspects of my Remembered, Reflected, and Programmed Identity are negatively impacting my private money-raising performance and results?*
   - Remembered identity—I have lost money in the past.
   - Reflective identity—Not being very focused on details, I have lost people's money. Also, I've never thought of myself as having a real job because I have not had a W-2 in years.
   - Programmed identity—In my life, I have not had any direct personal examples of wealth or people with wealth who I can relate to. So I really can't identify myself as having wealth or dealing with wealthy people.

2. *What do I currently believe about myself that is negatively impacting my raising private money performance and results?*
   - I feel uncomfortable with one-on-one conversations with private money sources and busy professionals about business and raising money.
   - I experience anxiety when talking to busy professionals when the conversation turns serious or related to business.
   - I don't see myself as being equal to wealthy people or even being someone that they will want to talk to.

3. *What would I like my raising private money identity to be?*

I am a powerful money magnet. I am so comfortable, confident, and at ease speaking with high net worth individuals and busy professionals. I am amazed at how much I love speaking one-on-one with high net worth individuals. I have a list of people who cannot wait to invest in my opportunities and make their money available to me for any future investments I have.

4. *Why do I want the raising private money identity that I just described? What will be achieved as a result of having my new private money-raising identity that I described?*

I have created a new raising private money identity because I am taking my business to the next level. The financial results I am achieving benefits my family. We are now placing all of our children in private school instead of only just two of them.

We are aggressively moving back to living the lifestyle that we both desire. We are living the lifestyle of the rich and famous. We are living a lifestyle of financial freedom, free from stress, and free from worry or doubt. We have the freedom to relax, to love, and to live curiously again.

Because of my new private-lending identity, living the lifestyle that we desire is the everyday norm for me and my family.

5. *Why is it important to achieve the private money-raising results that I have identified above?*

It is important that I achieve the raising private money financial results so that I can have the complete piece of mind that I've had in the past.

6. *How will achieving my private money goals positively impact my life and the lives of the people I care about?*

The positive impact on my life and my family's lives are many. We will all be more relaxed and happier. We will all be able to enjoy each moment with each other more fully.

We will be able to work and focus on work when it is time for work. And when it is time for play, we will focus on playing hard and enjoying it, without thinking about the work that we "should" be doing.

We will all have peace of mind, and we will be able to freely flow each and every day.

The positive impact on the lives of the people I care about will involve my being able to positively influence their lives financially. I will be able to assist in filling the financial gaps and empowering them to gain their own financial freedom.

7. *How will I feel when I have achieved my private money goals?*

I will feel magnificent! I know that I am in the right place, at the right time, doing the right thing. I will know that I will be able to maintain financial stability, regardless of what is going on in the market and with the economy.

I will know that I control my destiny because of my decisions and my actions.

I will feel grateful and proud because I am able to raise the amount of private money that I set as a goal.

I will feel optimistic because I know I'm able to positively control the amount of private money that I raise. Therefore, I will feel empowered to continually set higher and higher goals because my destiny is in my hands.

8. *What will be the negative consequences if I do not achieve the raising private money results that I desire?*

The negative consequences are that I would have failed. Therefore, my kids will not grow up in the positive environment that I had envisioned for them.

I wouldn't have the financial resources to support the people who I love and care about financially when they need it. As a result, I would feel sad, angry, and disappointed with myself.

I wouldn't be able to send my children to the right college or the right university that would have helped them discover and develop their true gifts and unique abilities.

9. *How would I feel if I did nothing differently than I am currently doing and my raising private money results remain exactly the same?*

If I did nothing differently, I would continue to feel the stress and continue to scramble. I would always be scrambling to meet that next financial obligation. I would not have the financial resources that I desire. I would not be able to "step into my greatness" and live the lifestyle that I so desperately desire.

I would feel very disappointed in myself.

I would feel angry because I know that my family would pay the price for my failure

10. *Given that I am committed to achieving my private money goals, what actions will I take to do so?*

The actions that I'm taking to meet my private money goals are to implement everything that I've learned from reading this book and completing the exercises in it.

I will develop a critical action plan with the action items I am going to implement, organized by the week and month that I am going to take that action.

I will review my results each week and make sure that I am removing any obstacles or barriers that are preventing me from implementing the items for my critical action plan.

11. *Read, visualize and experience my new identity statement three to six times a day.*

I will set a reminder into my phone to block one to five minutes to read, visualize, and experience my new private money-raising identity three to six times a day.

This is the end of the Creating a Winning Identity Exercise example.

Creating a Winning Identity Reflective Assessment Questions. Please answer the following questions on separate sheets of paper.

1. What aspects of my remembered, reflected, and programmed identity are negatively impacting my private money-raising performance and results?
   a. Remembered identity?
   b. Reflective identity?
   c. Programmed identity?
2. What do I currently believe about myself that is negatively impacting my private money-raising performance and results?
3. What would I like my private money-raising identity to be?
4. Why do I want the private money-raising identity that I just described? What will be achieved as a result of having my new private money-raising identity that I described?
5. Why is it important to achieve the private money-raising results that I have identified above?
6. How will achieving my private money goals positively impact my life and the lives of the people I care about?
7. How will I feel when I have achieved my private money goals?
8. What will be the negative consequences if I do not achieve the private money-raising results that I desire?
9. How would I feel if I did nothing differently than I am currently doing and my private money-raising results remained exactly the same?
10. Given that I am committed to achieving my private money goals, what actions will I take to do so?
11. Read, visualize, and experience my new identity statement three to six times a day.
12. Take action on the things that come to you as a result of your commitment to achieve your private money goal.
13. Repeat this process for any item or items of your identity, limiting beliefs, or negative behaviors that are not in alignment with achieving your private money goals.

Now that you have created your new winning identity, in the next chapter you will read the conclusion of *The Inner Game of Raising Private Money*.

CONCLUSION

AT ANY MOMENT IN YOUR life, you can truly take your private money-raising results to the next level. After reading this book, it is no longer a mystery or a secret about how to achieve breakthrough results with raising private money. The process is clear. You only have to implement the steps outlined in the private money-raising success formula, and you're well on your way to achieving exceptional results.

Remember, it is not what you know that determines your results, rather, it is how much of what you know that you're able to get yourself to implement that leads to extraordinary results. Focusing solely on the Outer Game is not sufficient for significantly increasing the amount of private money that you raise because all the strategies, techniques, and practices for raising private money that you're not able to get yourself to implement will not change your performance one iota.

You have the potential to raise all the private money you want, need, and desire. Now you have the raising private money success formula to help you turn that potential into results.

You have the formula to create a new private money-raising reality, and I am confident that you're well on your way to making your private money-raising dreams a reality.

The future is a creation, and you have the process for creating a new and different private money-raising future, one where you are consistently raising all the private money you need, want, and desire.

I will see you at the top!

EXERCISE ANSWERS

The Nine Dot Test

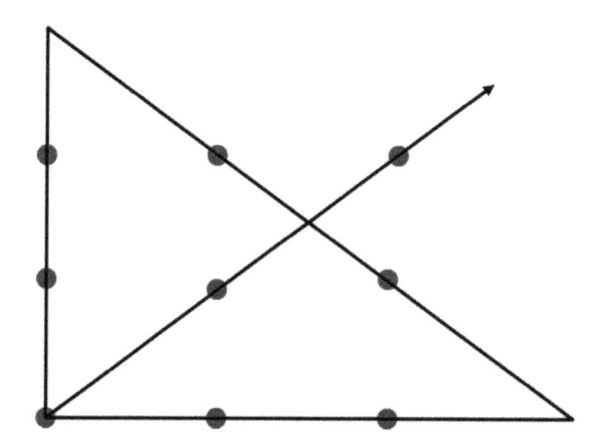

The "F" Exercise

- There are **7** total **f**'s in the exercise

> **F**inished **f**iles are the result o**f** years o**f** scientific study combined with the experience o**f** many years o**f** experts.

CPSIA information can be obtained
at www.ICGtesting.com
Printed in the USA
LVHW01s1704061117
555223LV00002B/177/P